MODEL JURY INSTRUCTIONS

SECOND EDITION

PATENT LITIGATION

EDITOR

Matt C. Acosta

AMERICAN BAR ASSOCIATION
Litigation Section

Cover design by ABA Design

Printed in the United States of America.

27 26 25 24 23 5 4 3 2 1

ISBN 978-1-63905-310-0

A catalog record for this book is available from the Library of Congress.

Contents

Drafting Committee

The following members of the American Bar Association Litigation Section's Committee on Intellectual Property Litigation participated in the preparation of these revised Model Jury Instructions for Patent Litigation.

Matt C. Acosta
Platt Cheema Richmond PLLC
Dallas, TX

Kristina R. Cary
Kirkland & Ellis LLP
Boston, MA

Marcus R. Chatterton
Balch & Bingham LLP
Birmingham, AL

John Kenneth Felter
Ropes & Gray LLP
Boston, MA

Noah Frank
Kirkland & Ellis LLP
Boston, MA

Jeanne M. Heffernan
Kirkland & Ellis LLP
Austin, TX

Tiffany M. Knapp
Kirkland & Ellis LLP
Boston, MA

Matthew A. Lembo
Perkins Coie
New York, NY

Andrew Lin
Platt Cheema Richmond PLLC
Dallas, TX

Vikram Mathrani
Honigman LLP
Chicago, IL

Michael Padden
Chicago, IL

Simon Safir
iLaw
Allen, TX

Daniel Sternberg
McDermott Will & Emery
Boston, MA

Joseph Van Tassel
Cooley LLP
Reston, VA

Foreword to Model Jury Instructions Series

Jury instructions: that is where the rubber hits the road in the law. At their best, jury instructions summarize cogently, clearly, and distinctly the contours of the law that a jury must apply to the facts. At their worst, jury instructions are tangled, arcane, incomprehensible legalese masquerading as a guide for the jury.

The jury instructions in this volume pertain to patent law litigation. They are for those among us who, every once in a while, fail to settle a case and therefore must go to trial. When a case is tried before a judge, that judge is presumed to know the law. When the case is tried before a jury of laypeople, they are presumed not to know the law. Therefore, they must be provided with a legal road map. These jury instructions are intended to serve that purpose. They can be used as such a guide not only in court before a jury, but also for evaluating and preparing a case for trial. These jury instructions are designed to tell a jury, and therefore you, what you must prove to prevail in your case. We hope you will find the guidance provided in this volume enlightening and useful at the multiple stages of taking, preparing, and trying a case.

Each jury instruction is intended to be party-neutral; however, because ours is an adversarial system of justice, lawyers may try to rewrite these neutral instructions in a manner that better presents the case for their clients. We wish those lawyers luck in convincing a court that the proposed reformulation conforms to the status of the law. Obviously, because the law is rarely static, the success of such reformulation will closely track any developments in the law.

In the notes that follow each instruction, you will find discussion of cases from which the instruction is derived, whether plaintiffs and defendants disagree on its use, and how it might be modified depending upon the individual circumstances.

These model jury instructions do not incorporate standard form instructions dealing with generalized burdens of proof, credibility of witnesses, or other such background matters that every set of jury instructions is presumed to include. These instructions do include instructions on a wide range of issues and causes of action that arise in the context of patent law litigation. The table of contents spells these out for the reader and is intended to assure ease of use.

As the Litigation Section of the American Bar Association, we can imagine few more useful tools to provide our colleagues than cogent, clear, and distinct jury instructions. We have designated these jury instructions as "model" ones because we hope that, in time, that is what they will become.

To that end, we invite the readers and users of these proposed model jury instructions to share their reactions with us. Let us know which of the instructions work and which do not. Let us know which of the instructions you believe could be more clearly written. Let us know which of the instructions a court has refused to give and why. In a future edition, we will try to incorporate your feedback so that these proposed "model" jury instructions in fact become model in use.

The feedback from judicial and practitioner users of our other model jury instructions has been positive indeed. We hope that this volume will be accorded the same acceptance received by our other jury instruction volumes. The profession certainly owes a large debt of gratitude to those individual lawyers who have given so unstintingly and so generously of their time to produce these jury instructions.

Book Publishing Board
Litigation Section

Introduction

In preparing these model patent jury instructions, we attempted to create a set of plain-English, party-neutral instructions that not only reflect the current state of the law, but are also simple and easy to understand. These instructions are written for jurors to understand and apply. Similarly, we have included sample verdict forms that are focused on simplicity to avoid issues that sometimes arise with complexity.

The instructions focus on the jury's role as fact-finder and the broad legal principles of patent law. They do not, however, address every factor or legal theory that courts have used to decide a particular issue. If such a factor or legal theory is relevant to a particular case, it may be addressed by a special instruction or through arguments made by trial counsel.

This revised edition includes additional instructions and sections that expand on previous versions of the instructions. For example, there are now separate instructions for pre- and post-America Invents Act standards for prior art, anticipation, and obviousness to account for patents with effective filing dates in either time period. This new edition also includes expanded sections on joint infringement, objective indicia of non-obviousness, and various individual factors for determining lost profits and reasonable royalties. Finally, we are pleased to include sample instructions regarding design patent infringement, invalidity, and damages.

The instructions are divided into two parts: preliminary instructions and final instructions. Preliminary jury instructions are an important tool in aiding jurors with their fact-finding role. Jurors in civil trials are presented with enormous amounts of unfamiliar and often extremely complex information. This is especially true in patent cases, where jurors must grapple with a unique field of law and factual subject matter that often involves sophisticated technology.

Preliminary instructions provide the framework within which jurors may process and filter the information they receive. The preliminary instructions introduce to the jury the factual and legal framework within which the trial will take place, and explain what will be expected of them, all before they hear any evidence. This facilitates jury comprehension and retention of the information the jurors receive at trial.

The final instructions included here encompass the major issues that arise in patent litigation. Because every issue does not arise in every case, each instruction is designed to stand on its own, enabling the user to pick and choose the instructions relevant to the case. The instructions assume the more common situation in a patent infringement case, i.e., a suit in which the plaintiff is enforcing the patent(s)-in-suit against the accused infringer, but may be easily modified for use in declaratory judgment actions, where the plaintiff is accused of infringing the defendant's patent.

The final instructions include notes and authorities. The notes discuss current developments in patent law and potential issues that may arise requiring additional instruction, and they identify areas where potential conflicts exist in the case law. The authorities include a sample of relevant case law supporting the instructions and generally include the leading cases on fundamental and important principles.

Chapter One

PRELIMINARY INSTRUCTIONS

1.1 Introduction

Now that you have been sworn in, I have the following preliminary instructions for guidance on your role as jurors in this case. This is an action for patent infringement arising under the patent laws of the United States. I now want to briefly tell you what this case is about. This case involves a dispute relating to (asserted patent(s)). Before summarizing the positions of the parties and the issues involved in the dispute, I will take a moment to explain what a patent is and how one is obtained.

1.2 What Is a U.S. Patent and How Is One Obtained?

Patents are granted by the United States Patent and Trademark Office (sometimes called the USPTO or PTO). A valid United States patent gives the patent holder the right to prevent others from making, using, offering to sell, or selling the patented invention within the United States, or from importing it into the United States, without the patent holder's permission. A violation of the patent holder's rights is called infringement. The patent holder may try to enforce a patent against persons it believes to be infringers by a lawsuit filed in federal court. A United States patent is valid for up to 20 years from the date the patent application was filed.

The process of obtaining a patent is called patent prosecution. To obtain a patent, an inventor must first file an application with the USPTO. The USPTO is an agency of the United States Government and employs trained examiners who review applications for patents. The application includes a section that is called a "specification." The specification contains a written description of the claimed invention telling what the invention is, how it works, how to make it, and how to use it. The specification ends with one or more numbered sentences. These numbered sentences are the patent "claims." Each claim consists of one or more clauses called "limitations," which set forth the specific requirements of the claim. Each limitation contains one or more distinct components called "elements." [IF METHOD PATENT: Each "limitation" of a method patent claim contains one or more "steps" for performing the function or desired result of the claim.] When the patent is eventually granted by the USPTO, the claims define the boundaries of the patent's protection and give notice to the public of those boundaries. Issued patents (and published patent applications) are public records that can be searched and reviewed by anyone who cares to do so.

An examiner reviews the filed application to determine whether or not the claims are patentable (that is to say, appropriate for patent protection) and whether or not the specification adequately describes the invention claimed. In examining a patent application, the examiner reviews certain information about the state of the technology at the time the application was filed. This type of information is called "prior art." The USPTO searches for and reviews prior art that is publicly available or has been submitted by the applicant.

The examiner reviews this prior art to determine whether or not the invention is truly an advance over the state of the art at the time the application was filed. Prior art is defined by law, and I will later give you specific instructions as to what constitutes prior art. In general, though, prior art includes information that demonstrates the state of the technology that existed before the claimed invention was made or before the application for a patent was filed. A patent lists the prior art that was cited, either by the applicant or the examiner. The items on this list are called the "cited references."

After the prior art search and examination of the application, the examiner informs the applicant in writing of what the examiner has found and whether the examiner considers any claim to be patentable and, thus, "allowed." This is called an "Office Action." However, if the examiner rejects the claims, the applicant has an opportunity to respond to the examiner to try to persuade the examiner to allow the claims.

The applicant also has the chance to change the claims or to submit new claims, and this process may go back and forth between the applicant and the examiner for some time until the examiner is satisfied that the application meets the requirements for a patent. And in that case, the application issues as a United States patent. Or, in the alternative, if the examiner ultimately concludes that the application should be rejected, then no patent will issue.

[IF CONTINUATION: The applicant may also file what are called continuation applications, which are subsequent applications with the same disclosure as an earlier-filed application but which list different claims and may result in a different, later issued patent.]

[IF CONTINUATION-IN-PART: The applicant may also file what are called continuation-in-part applications, which are subsequent applications that include the disclosure of an earlier-filed application as well as additional disclosure that was subsequently added.]

The papers generated during the communications back and forth between the examiner and the applicant are called the "prosecution history."

[IF INVALIDITY IS ALLEGED: The fact that the USPTO grants a patent does not necessarily mean that any invention claimed in the patent, in fact, deserves the protection of a patent. For example, the USPTO may not have had available to it all other prior art that will be presented to you. A party accused of infringement has the right to argue here in federal court that a claimed invention in the patent is invalid because it does not meet the requirements for a patent. It is your job as the jury to consider the evidence presented by the parties and determine independently whether or not (accused infringer) has proven that the patent is invalid.]

[IF DESIGN PATENT: An applicant may also obtain patent protection for a design. Unlike utility patents, a design patent can have only one claim. That claim covers all the figures in the patent. It is permissible to illustrate more than one embodiment of a design in a single-design patent application. Each design patent contains multiple drawings to illustrate the claimed design. The scope of the claim encompasses the design's visual appearance as a whole. It does not cover a general design concept and is not limited to isolated features of the drawings. All matter depicted in solid lines in the drawing contributes to the overall appearance of the design. Any portion of the drawing that is depicted in dashed lines is outside the scope of the claimed design.]

1.3 Summary of the Parties' Contentions

The case involves United States Patent No(s). [ ], obtained by (inventor), and is now owned by (patent holder). For your convenience, the parties and I will often refer to this patent number (full patent number) by the last three numbers of the patent number, namely, as the (last three numbers of the patent) patent. (Patent holder) filed suit in this court seeking money damages from (alleged infringer) for allegedly infringing the [ ] patent by [making] [importing] [using] [selling] [offering for sale] [supplying or causing to be supplied in or from the United States all or a substantial portion of the components of a patented invention] [in] [into] [within] the United States [products] [methods] [products that are made by a process patented in the United States] that (patent holder) argues are covered by claims [ ] of the [ ] patent.

[IF INDIRECT INFRINGEMENT ALLEGED: (Patent holder) also argues that (alleged infringer) has [actively induced infringement of these claims of the [ ] patent by others] [and] [or] [contributed to the infringement of claims [ ] of the [ ] patent by others].

The [products] [methods] that are alleged to infringe are (list of accused products or methods). (Alleged infringer) denies that it has infringed claims [ ] of the [ ] patent. (Alleged infringer) also argues that claims [ ] are invalid. I will instruct you later as to the ways in which a patent may be invalid. In general, however, a patent is invalid if it is not new or is obvious in view of the state of the art at the relevant time, or if the description in the patent does not meet certain requirements. (Add other defenses, if applicable.)

Your job will be to decide whether or not claims [ ] of the [ ] patent have been infringed and whether or not those claims are invalid. If you decide that any claim of the [ ] patent has been infringed and is not invalid, you will then need to decide any money damages to be awarded to [patent holder] to compensate it for the infringement.

[IF WILLFULNESS ALLEGED: You will also need to make a finding as to whether the infringement was willful. If you decide that any infringement was willful, that decision should not affect any damages award you give. I will take willfulness into account later.]

1.4 Summary of Applicable Law

In deciding the issues that are before you, you'll be asked to consider specific legal rules. I will give you an overview of those rules now, and then I will give you much more detailed instructions later.

My job in this case is to tell you what the law is, handle the procedure, and oversee the conduct of the trial as efficiently and effectively as possible. In determining the law, it is specifically my job to determine the meaning of any words or phrases in the numbered claims of the [ ] patent(s) that need interpretation. You must accept the meanings that I give you and use those meanings when you decide whether any particular claim has or has not been infringed and whether or not any claim is invalid. You will be given a document in a moment that reflects those meanings, which I have determined.

Also, for any claim term for which I have not provided you with the definition, you should apply the plain and ordinary meaning of that term. But if I have provided you with a definition, then you are to apply my definitions to those terms throughout the case.

Nonetheless, my interpretation of the language of the claims should not be taken by you as an indication that I have a personal opinion or any opinion at all regarding the issues, such as infringement and invalidity. Those issues are yours alone to decide.

1.4.1 Infringement

Infringement is decided on a claim-by-claim basis. Therefore, there may be infringement of one claim but no infringement of another. There are also a few different ways that a patent may be infringed. I will explain the requirements for each of these types of infringement to you in detail at the conclusion of the case. In general, however, a party may infringe the asserted patents by making, using, selling, or offering for sale a product in the United States, or by using a method meeting all the requirements of a claim of the asserted patent. I will provide you with more detailed instructions on the requirements for infringement at the conclusion of the case.

1.4.2 Invalidity

The second issue you are going to be asked to decide is whether the asserted patents are invalid. A patent may be invalid for a number of reasons, including because it claims subject matter that is not new or is obvious in light of what came before. That which came before is referred to as the "prior art." For a claim to be invalid because it is not new, (alleged infringer) must show that all of the limitations of a claim are present in a single prior device or method, or sufficiently described in a single prior printed publication or patent that qualifies as "prior art." If a claim is not new, it is said to be "anticipated" by the prior art.

Another way that a claim may be found to be invalid is that it may have been obvious. Even though every element of a claim is not shown or sufficiently described in a single piece of "prior art," the claim may still be invalid if it would have been obvious to a person of ordinary skill in the field of technology of the patent at the relevant time.

[IF WRITTEN DESCRIPTION OR ENABLEMENT DEFENSE ALLEGED: A patent may also be invalid if the "written description" in the specification does not meet certain requirements. In order to meet this written description requirement, the description of the invention in the patent's specification must be detailed enough to show that the inventor actually possessed the invention as broadly as claimed in the claims of the issued patent. The disclosure of a patent must also meet the "enablement" requirement. To meet this requirement, the description in the patent has to be sufficiently full and clear to have allowed, or "enabled," persons of ordinary skill in the field of technology of the patent to make and use the invention without undue experimentation at the time the patent application was originally filed.]

1.4.3 Damages

If you decide that any claim of the [ ] patent has been infringed and is not invalid, you will then need to determine any money damages to be awarded to (patent holder) to compensate it for the infringement. A damages award should be adequate to compensate for the infringement, but in no event may the damages award be less than what (patent holder) would have received had it been paid a reasonable royalty. I will instruct you later on the meaning of a reasonable royalty. Any damages you award are meant to compensate (patent holder) and not to punish (alleged infringer). You may not include in your award any additional amount as a fine or penalty, above what is necessary to compensate (patent holder) for the infringement, in order to punish (alleged infringer). I will give you more detailed instructions on the calculation of damages at the conclusion of the case.

1.5 Outline of Trial and Burdens of Proof

You are going to be hearing from a number of witnesses, and I want you to keep an open mind while you're listening to the evidence and not decide the facts until you have heard all the evidence. There are two types of evidence—direct evidence and circumstantial evidence. Direct evidence is direct proof of a fact, such as testimony by a witness about what that witness personally saw or heard or did. For example, a witness may testify that it was sunny when she arrived at the courthouse. Circumstantial evidence is proof of one or more facts from which you could find another fact. For example, if a witness testifies the skies were overcast and she saw puddles on the sidewalk, that may be circumstantial evidence that it had rained. You should consider both kinds of evidence. The law makes no distinction between the weight to be given to either direct or circumstantial evidence. It is for you to decide how much weight to give to any evidence. While the witnesses are testifying, remember that you and you alone will also have to decide the degree of credibility and believability to allocate to the witness and the evidence.

So while these witnesses are testifying, you should be asking yourself questions such as these:

- Does the witness impress you as being truthful?
- Does the witness have a reason not to tell the truth?
- Does the witness have any personal interest in the outcome of the case?
- Does the witness seem to have a good memory?
- Did the witness have an opportunity and ability to observe accurately the things [he] [she] testified about?
- Did the witness appear to understand the questions clearly and answer them directly?
- And, of course, does the testimony of the witness differ from that of another witness? If it does, how does it differ?

Now I want to give you my final instructions before we hear the opening statements from the lawyers. Each side is going to make an opening statement in just a moment. You need to understand that each side's opening statement is not evidence. It is simply their explanation of what they hope and expect the evidence will show.

The evidence in this case is the sworn testimony of the witnesses together with the exhibits that are admitted into evidence for your consideration. That and that alone is the evidence in this case.

There are two standards of proof that you will apply to the evidence, depending on the issue you are deciding.

As the jury, you will apply the burden of proof known as a *preponderance of the evidence* as well as a different burden of proof known as *clear and convincing evidence*. When a party has the burden of proof by a preponderance of the evidence, this means that you, the jury, must be persuaded by the evidence that a fact is more probably true than not true.

On the other hand, when a party has the burden of proof as to any defense by clear and convincing evidence, it means you, the jury, must have an abiding conviction that a fact is highly probable. That's a higher standard of proof than the preponderance of the evidence.

Now, neither of these burdens of proof is to be confused with a different burden of proof called *beyond a reasonable doubt.* That burden is only used in a criminal case and it has no application in a civil case such as this, so you should not confuse clear and convincing evidence with beyond a reasonable doubt. Clear and convincing evidence is not as high as beyond a reasonable doubt, but it is higher than a preponderance of the evidence.

Before we get started with opening statements, I want to give you a brief roadmap of how the trial will be conducted and what you should expect.

[Note: ADJUST ORDER ACCORDINGLY IF DECLARATORY JUDGMENT ACTION FILED BY ALLEGED INFRINGER.] After the opening statements, (patent holder) will present its evidence in support of its contentions that several claims of the asserted patents have been infringed by (alleged infringer) [and that such infringement has been willful]. To prove infringement of any claim, (patent holder) must persuade you that it is more likely than not that (alleged infringer) has infringed that claim; that is, (patent holder) must prove infringement by a preponderance of the evidence. [(Patent holder) must also prove that the infringement was willful by a preponderance of the evidence.] As part of its case, (patent holder) will also present to you evidence on the amount of damages that it contends it is entitled to due to the alleged infringement. (Patent holder) must also prove the amount of damages by a preponderance of the evidence.

Now, after (patent holder) has presented its evidence and rests, then (alleged infringer) will present its evidence that the asserted claims of (asserted patent(s)) are invalid. To prove invalidity of any claim, (alleged infringer) must persuade you by clear and convincing evidence that the claims are invalid.

(Alleged infringer) will also put on evidence responding to (patent holder's) proof as to infringement and damages.

Now, after (alleged infringer) presents its evidence and rests its case, (patent holder) may then put on additional evidence responding to (alleged infringer's) evidence that the claims of (asserted patent(s)) are invalid and to offer additional evidence of infringement and damages. This is referred to as rebuttal evidence, and that portion of the case is often called the rebuttal portion of the case. (Patent holder's) rebuttal evidence may respond to any evidence offered by (alleged infringer).

[Note: ADJUST ORDER ACCORDINGLY BASED ON JUDGE'S PREFERRED ORDER AND WHETHER A REBUTTAL ON INVALIDITY WILL BE OFFERED AFTER THE PLAINTIFF RESTS.] After the rebuttal case is put on and the parties have rested, then all the evidence will have been presented, and at that time, I will give you final instructions in this case. Then the lawyers will present their closing arguments to the jury. After that, you will retire to the jury room to deliberate and reach your unanimous verdict in this case.

Chapter Two

INFRINGEMENT

2.1 Patent Infringement Generally; Direct Infringement

A patent owner has the right to stop others from using the invention covered by its patent claims during the life of the patent. A person infringes a patent by making, using, selling, or offering to sell [or importing] what is covered by the patent claims without the patent owner's permission. This type of infringement is called "direct infringement." [In addition to enforcing a patent against a direct infringer, a patent owner also has the right to enforce the patent against those who are known as "indirect infringers."]

Only the claims of a patent can be infringed. You must compare the (asserted claims) as I have defined them, to the accused [product] [process], and determine whether or not there is infringement. You should not compare (alleged infringer's) [product] [process] with any specific example set out in the patent, or with (patent holder's) [product] [process]. The only correct comparison is with the language of the claim itself, with the meaning I have given you.

You must consider each claim individually and must reach your decision as to each assertion of infringement based on my instructions about the meaning and scope of the claims, the legal requirements for infringement, and the evidence presented to you by the parties. I will first discuss direct infringement.

Whether or not (alleged infringer) knew that what it was doing was an infringement does not matter. A person may directly infringe a patent even if he or she believed in good faith that what he or she was doing was not an infringement of any patent, and even if he or she did not know of the patent.

In this case, (patent holder) asserts that (alleged infringer's) [product] [process] directly infringes (asserted claims) of (asserted patent(s)). It is your job to determine whether (patent holder) has proved by a preponderance of the evidence that (alleged infringer) has directly infringed any of (asserted claims) of (asserted patent(s)).

Authorities

35 U.S.C. §§ 271–81; *Warner-Jenkinson Co. v. Hilton Davis Chem. Co.*, 520 U.S. 17, 36 (1997); *Fla. Prepaid Postsecondary Educ. Expense Bd. v. College Sav. Bank*, 527 U.S. 627, 644 (1999); *DeMarini Sports, Inc. v. Worth, Inc.*, 239 F.3d 1314, 1330 (Fed. Cir. 2001); *Payless Shoesource, Inc. v. Reebok Int'l Ltd.*, 998 F.2d 985, 990 (Fed. Cir. 1993); *Atl. Thermoplastics Co. v. Faytex Corp.*, 974 F.2d 1299, 1300 (Fed. Cir. 1992); *Intel Corp. v. Int'l Trade Comm'n*, 946 F.2d 821, 832 (Fed. Cir.1991); *High Tech Med. Instrumentation, Inc. v. New Image Indus., Inc.*, 49 F.3d 1551, 1554–55 (Fed. Cir. 1995); *Nobelpharma AB v. Nobelpharma USA, Inc.*, 141 F.3d 1059, 1067–68 (Fed. Cir. 1998).

2.1.1 Literal Infringement

In order to literally infringe a patent claim, a [product] [process] must include every limitation of the claim. If (alleged infringer's) [product] [process] omits even a single [element] [step] recited in a claim, then you must find that (alleged infringer) has not infringed that claim. You must consider each of the patent claims separately.

A claim limitation is present in an accused [product] [process] if it exists in the [product] [process] just as it is described in the claim language, either as I have explained that language to you or, if I did not explain it, as you understand it.

Note

This instruction should be used with an added instruction for the doctrine of equivalents if both literal infringement and infringement under the doctrine of equivalents are at issue in the case.

Authorities

Intellectual Sci. & Tech. v. Sony Elec., 589 F.3d 1179, 1183 (Fed. Cir. 2009); *Hutchins v. Zoll Med. Corp.*, 492 F.3d 1377, 1380 (Fed. Cir. 2007); *Rosco, Inc. v. Mirror Lite Co.*, 304 F.3d 1373, 1378–79 (Fed. Cir. 2002); *PHG Tech., LLC v. St. John Co.*, 469 F.3d 1361, 1369 (Fed. Cir. 2006); *Tate Access Floors, Inc. v. Interface Architectural Res.*, 279 F.3d 1357, 1366 (Fed. Cir. 2002) (citing *Baxter Healthcare Corp. v. Spectramed, Inc.*, 48 F.3d 1575, 1582–83 (Fed. Cir. 1995)); *Smith & Nephew, Inc. v. Ethicon, Inc.*, 276 F.3d 1304, 1311 (Fed. Cir. 2001); *Teva Pharm. USA, Inc. v. Sandoz, Inc.*, 574 U.S. 318 (2015).

2.1.2 Joint Infringement

In this case, (alleged infringer) is accused of direct infringement. (Alleged infringer) asserts that it has not directly infringed (asserted patent(s)) because it did not perform each step of a claimed method or did not perform all the steps necessary to make, sell, offer for sale, or import (allegedly infringing product) because (another party) performed one of more of the acts necessary to infringe. If you find that one or more of the steps performed by another party cannot be attributed to (alleged infringer), then you must find that there is no joint infringement. In determining whether the steps are attributable to (alleged infringer), you should consider whether (alleged infringer) exercised direction or control over (the other party) when it performed these acts, whether (alleged infringer) and (the other party) have a contract that requires (the other party) to perform [a step] [steps] of the claimed method on (alleged infringer's) behalf, or whether (alleged infringer) made participation in an activity or receipt of a benefit by (the third party) conditioned upon performance of [a step] [steps] of the patented method and established when (the third party) would perform the [step] [steps].

Additionally, if you find that a joint enterprise performed all the acts of infringement, then all participants in the joint enterprise are liable for infringement. A joint enterprise exists if you find: (1) an agreement, express or implied, existed among the member of the group; (2) the group had a common purpose; (3) the members of the group had a community of pecuniary interest; and (4) all members had an equal right to voice direction of the group and equal control.

Note

This instruction reflects the most recent case law but should be checked for all future use. This area of patent law has been the subject of numerous Federal Circuit and Supreme Court decisions and is still evolving.

Authorities

Akamai Tech., Inc. v. Limelight Networks, Inc., 797 F.3d 1020 (Fed. Cir. 2015) (en banc); *Eli Lilly & Co. v. Teva Parenteral Meds., Inc.*, 845 F.3d 1357, 1364–67 (Fed. Cir. 2017); *Limelight Networks, Inc. v. Akamai Tech.*, Inc., 572 U.S. 915 (2014); *Travel Sentry, Inc. v. Tropp*, 877 F.3d 1370 1377–80 (Fed. Cir. 2017).

2.1.3 Infringement; Doctrine of Equivalents

A claim limitation is present in an accused [product] [process] under the doctrine of equivalents if the differences between the claim limitation and a comparable element of the accused [product] [process] are insubstantial. One way to determine this is to look at whether the accused [product] [process] performs substantially the same function, in substantially the same way, to achieve substantially the same result as the claimed invention.

Another way to determine whether the differences are insubstantial is to consider whether or not people of ordinary skill in the field of the invention believe that the [structure] [step] of the accused [product] [process] and the [structure] [step] recited in the patent claim limitation are interchangeable. A person of ordinary skill is a person with average education and training in the field. The belief of such a person must be based on what was known at the time of the activities that constitute the alleged infringement, and not what was known at the time the patent application was filed or when the patent issued. Thus, the inventor need not have foreseen, and the patent need not describe, all potential equivalents to the invention covered by the claims. Also, slight changes in technique or improvements made possible by technology developed after the patent application is filed may still be considered equivalent for the purposes of the doctrine of equivalents.

The same [element] [method] [step] of the accused [product] [method] may satisfy more than one element of a claim. If you find that all of the remaining elements of the claim are present in the accused [product] [method] and that these differences are insubstantial, you may find infringement under the doctrine of equivalents. Also, two [elements] [methods] of the accused [product] [method] may satisfy a single claim element.

[The following paragraph should be used in addition to the above paragraphs in cases involving chemical compounds or chemical compositions.]:

As I have explained to you, (asserted claims) of (asserted patent(s)) are directed to a chemical compound or composition made up of certain listed ingredients. If you find that the accused product does not literally include every limitation of these claims because of changes to one or more of the ingredients, you may use another test to decide whether the changed ingredient is equivalent to the ingredient listed in the claim. That test is whether or not the changed ingredient has the same purpose, quality, and function as the claimed ingredient. In other words, you must consider whether the new ingredient in the accused product and the ingredient listed in the claim serve the same purpose, have the same qualities when combined with the other ingredients of the chemical compound or composition, and perform the same function.

Note

This instruction should be used with the instruction on literal infringement when infringement under the doctrine of equivalents is an issue in the case, either alone or with a claim of literal infringement.

In *Warner-Jenkinson Co. v. Hilton-Davis Chem. Co.*, 520 U.S. 17 (1997), the Supreme Court confirmed the viability of the doctrine of equivalents as a basis for an infringement finding. The Court also confirmed the standard to be used for determining whether or not an accused product or process contains an element or step that is equivalent to a claim limitation. *Id.* at 27.

An element or step is equivalent to a claim limitation if the differences between that element or step and the claim limitation are insubstantial. *Id.* at 40. The Supreme Court has left it to the Federal Circuit to identify specific tests to be used in determining whether or not such differences are insubstantial. *Id.*

This instruction sets out the most commonly used "function-way-result" and "known interchangeability" tests for infringement under the doctrine of equivalents. *Id.* at 25; *see also Graver Tank & Mfg. Co. v. Linde Air Prods. Co.*, 339 U.S. 605, 609 (1950). It also sets out the "purpose, quality and function" test used with claims directed to chemical compositions. *Warner-Jenkinson*, 520 U.S. at 25; *see also Graver Tank*, 339 U.S. at 609. Left for the argument of counsel are the factors that have been identified in the case law for determining the range of equivalents to which the claim limitations are entitled.

Authorities

Warner-Jenkinson Co. v. Hilton Davis Chem. Co., 520 U.S. 17, 37 (1997); *Graver Tank & Mfg. Co. v. Linde Air Prods. Co.*, 339 U.S. 605, 609 (1950); *Advanceme Inc. v. Rapidpay LLC*, 509 F. Supp. 2d 593, 606 (E.D. Tex. 2007); *Allen Eng'g Corp. v. Bartell Indus., Inc.*, 299 F.3d 1336, 1351 (Fed. Cir. 2002); *Riles v. Shell Exploration & Prod. Co.*, 298 F.3d 1302, 1309–10 (Fed. Cir. 2002); *DeMarini Sports, Inc. v. Worth, Inc.*, 239 F.3d 1314, 1331–34 (Fed. Cir. 2001); *Biovail Corp. Int'l v. Andrx Pharms., Inc.*, 239 F.3d 1297,1302–03 (Fed. Cir. 2001); *Teva Pharm, USA, Inc. v. Sandoz, Inc.*, 810 F. Supp. 2d 578, 592 (S.D.N.Y. 2011); *Moore U.S.A., Inc. v. Standard Register Co.*, 229 F.3d 1091, 1107 (Fed. Cir. 2000); *Cadence Pharm., Inc. v. Exela Pharmsci Inc.*, 780 F.3d 1364, 1372 (Fed. Cir. 2015); *Advanced Display Sys., Inc. v. Kent State Univ.*, 212 F.3d 1272, 1287 (Fed. Cir. 2000); *Bayer AG v. Elan Pharm. Research Corp.*, 212 F.3d 1241, 1247–50 (Fed. Cir. 2000); *Ferring B.V. v. Watson Labs, Inc.*, 764 F.3d 1401, 1408–09 (Fed.

Cir. 2014); *Augustine Med., Inc. v. Gaymar Indus., Inc.*, 181 F.3d 1291, 1301–02 (Fed. Cir. 1999); *Cardinal Chem. Co. v. Morton Int'l, Inc.*, 508 U.S. 83 (1993).

2.1.4 Limitations on the Doctrine of Equivalents

The patent law places certain limits on the doctrine of equivalents. It is my duty to decide whether or not any of these limits apply in this case and to instruct you on my decision. You must follow my instruction in considering both infringement and invalidity issues.

One limit on the doctrine of equivalents occurs as the result of changes to the patent claims or arguments that the patent owner made in order to obtain [his] [her] patent. A patent owner may not include within the patent claims [products] [processes] that [he] [she] gave up in order to obtain [his] [her] patent.

In this case, the following limits apply to the claims of (asserted patent(s)).

[Court to supply any prosecution history estoppel only if the Court determines as a matter of law that the instruction applies.]:

In this case, I have determined, as a matter of law, that the doctrine of equivalents cannot be applied to certain elements of the asserted claims. I am instructing you that the following elements cannot be considered as having equivalents:

[List Elements on a claim-by-claim basis.]

Consequently, each of the elements above must be literally present within (alleged infringer's) [product] [method] for there to be infringement of the claim. As for the remaining elements of the asserted claims not listed above, you are permitted to find these elements with the doctrine of equivalents analysis that I instructed you on earlier.

Another limit on the doctrine of equivalents occurs when the patent specification describes a specific role or function for a claim limitation. When this occurs, any equivalent structure must fill substantially the same role as that described in the patent specification for that limitation. In this case, this limit applies as follows:

[Court to supply any such limit.]

Additionally, if a patent discloses subject matter but does not include it within its claims, the patentee has dedicated that unclaimed subject matter to the public. If (the patent) discloses, but does not claim, subject matter alleged to be equivalent to an element of the patent claim, then the [component] [step] alleged to be equivalent in (alleged infringer's) [product] [method] cannot be an equivalent to that element of the patent claim for purposes of infringement under the doctrine of equivalents. This is true even if the failure to claim the subject matter was wholly unintentional. In this case, you are instructed that subject matter from the patent has been dedicated to the public and the doctrine of equivalents analysis cannot be applied to the following elements of the asserted claims:

[List elements on a claim-by-claim basis.]

Unless each of these elements is literally present within (alleged infringer's) [product] [method], there can be no infringement of the claim.

Authorities

Festo Corp. v. Shoketsu Kinzoku Kogyo Kabushiki Co., 535 U.S. 722 (2002); *Warner-Jenkinson Co. v. Hilton Davis Chem. Co.*, 520 U.S. 17, 30–34 (1997); *Festo Corp. v. Shoketsu Kinzoku Kogyo Kabushiki Co.*, 344 F.3d 1359, 1366–67 (Fed. Cir. 2003) (en banc). *Pfizer, Inc. v. Teva Pharm.*, USA, Inc., 429 F.3d 1364, 1378–79 (Fed. Cir. 2005); *Toro Co. v. White Consol. Indus., Inc.*, 383 F.3d 1326 (Fed. Cir. 2004); *Newell Operating Co. v. Intercrown USA*, No. 06 CV 06050241, 2008 WL 5760155, at *13 (N.D. Ill., May 5, 2008); *Johnson & Johnston Assocs., Inc. v. R.E. Serv. Co.*, 285 F.3d 1046, 1054–55 (Fed. Cir. 2002) (en banc).

2.1.5 Infringement; Means-Plus-Function or Step-Plus-Function Claim Limitations

A [means-plus-function] [step-plus-function] claim limitation describes a means for performing a particular function. To prove that an accused product includes a [structure] [act] that is covered by a means-plus-function limitation, a patent owner must prove two things by a preponderance of the evidence: first, that the accused [product] [process] contains a [structure] [act] that performs the identical function to the function recited in the means-plus-function limitation; and second, that the [structure] [act] of the accused [product] [process] that performs that function is either identical or equivalent to the corresponding [structure] [act] disclosed in the patent specification.

Whether or not the [structure] [act] of the accused [product] [process] is equivalent to the [structure] [act] disclosed in the patent is decided from the perspective of a person of ordinary skill in the field of the invention. A person of ordinary skill is a person of average education and training in the field. A structure is equivalent if such an ordinary skilled person would consider the differences between the accused [structure] [act] and the [structure] [act] in the patent to be insubstantial.

One way of determining whether the [structure] [act] of the accused [product] [process] is equivalent to the [structure] [act] disclosed in the specification is to determine whether or not persons of ordinary skill in the field of the invention believe that the [structure] [act] disclosed in the specification and the [structure] [act] of the accused [product] [process] are interchangeable. Another way is to determine whether or not the accused [structure] [act] performs the identical function, in substantially the same way, to achieve substantially the same result, as the [structure] [act] disclosed in the specification.

Let's use an example of a claim reciting three limitations—first, a tabletop; second, legs; and third, a means for securing the legs to the tabletop. The third limitation is the means-plus-function portion of the claim. The patent specification in our example discloses glue to secure the legs to the tabletop. Let's assume that the accused device uses nails. They both perform the claimed function of securing the legs to the tabletop. The fact that nails and glue are different does not mean that, under the patent laws, they may not be equivalent. Whether or not they are equivalent depends on such things as whether the glue is important to the invention claimed in the patent, whether those skilled in the art of table-making would consider the glue and nails to be interchangeable, and whether in the patent or prosecution history the two are referred to as equivalent.

Equivalency is determined as of the issuance of the patent, in this case (date). In deciding whether or not a structure in (alleged infringer's) product is included in the means-plus-function limitation of claims [ ] of the [ ] patent, you must first decide whether or not the technology used in the structure of (alleged infringer's) product that relates to the means-plus-function limitation was known on the date the [ ] patent issued. Under the patent laws, a structure that incorporates technology that was developed after the issuance of the patent cannot be literally included in the means-plus-function limitations of that patent.

Thus, if you find that the technology incorporated in the structure of (alleged infringer's) product was developed after the [ ] patent issued, then you can only consider whether or not the means-plus-function limitations of the [ ] patent claims are included in (alleged infringer's) product under the doctrine of equivalents.

Note

This instruction should be used when infringement under the doctrine of equivalents is not an issue with respect to a means-plus-function limitation. Determining whether or not a disclosed structure corresponds to the function recited in a means-plus-function limitation involves a question of law for the court.

Authorities

35 U.S.C. § 112; *Williamson v. Citrix Online, LLC*, 792 F.3d 1339, 1349 (Fed. Cir. 2015) (en banc); *J&M Corp.* v. *Harley-Davidson, Inc.*, 269 F.3d 1360, 1367 (Fed. Cir. 2001); *Medtronic, Inc.* v. *Advanced Cardiovascular Sys., Inc.*, 248 F.3d 1303, 1311 (Fed. Cir. 2001); *IMS Tech., Inc.* v. *Haas Automation, Inc.*, 206 F.3d 1422, 1435–37 (Fed. Cir. 2000); *Fast Memory Erase v. Intel Corp.*, Nos. 2010-1302, 2010-1324, 2011 WL 65460, at *1 (Fed. Cir. 2011); *Caterpillar Inc.* v. *Deere & Co.*, 224 F.3d 1374, 1380 (Fed. Cir. 2000); *Odetics, Inc.* v. *Storage Tech. Corp.*, 185 F.3d 1259, 1266–68 (Fed. Cir. 1999); *WMS Gaming Inc.* v. *Int'l Game Tech.*, 184 F.3d 1339, 1347–50 (Fed. Cir. 1999); *Al-Site Corp.* v. *VSI Int'l, Inc.*, 174 F.3d 1308,

1318–21 (Fed. Cir. 1999); *KSR Int'l Co. v. Telefax Inc.*, 550 U.S. 398 (2007); *Chiuminatta Concrete Concepts, Inc.* v. *Cardinal Indus., Inc.*, 145 F.3d 1303, 1307–10 (Fed. Cir. 1998); *Kraft Foods, Inc. v. Int'l Trading Co.*, 203 F.3d 1362 (Fed. Cir. 2000); *Wenger Mfg., Inc. v. Coating Mach. Sys., Inc.*, 239 F.3d 1225 (Fed. Cir. 2001); *B. Braun Med. Inc.* v. *Abbott Labs.*, 124 F.3d 1419, 1424–25 (Fed. Cir. 1997); *Alpex Computer Corp.* v. *Nintendo* Co., 102 F.3d 1214, 1221 (Fed. Cir. 1996); *Ind. Mills & Mfg. Inc. v. Dorel Indus., Inc.*, 369 F. Supp. 2d 1010, 1020–23 (S.D. Ind. 2005).

2.1.6 The Experimental Use Exception

The patent law regards the use of a [product] [process] for an experimental purpose differently from use for a commercial purpose. Thus, the law provides an exception to infringement when the accused [product] [process] was used strictly for experimental purposes. This is known as the "experimental use exception."

The experimental use exception permits someone to use a [product] [process] covered by a patent without the patent owner's permission, as long as the use is merely for philosophical experiments, or to determine whether a [product] [process] will work for its intended purpose. Such uses do not infringe a patent. Where, however, a use is in connection with a commercial purpose, the experimental use exception does not apply and the use will be an infringement.

(Alleged infringer) asserts that its use of the accused [product] [process] falls within the experimental use exception and, therefore, does not infringe (asserted claims) of (asserted patent(s)). If you find that (alleged infringer's) use of the accused [product] [process] was merely for philosophical purposes, or to determine whether the accused [product] [process] will work for its intended purpose, then you should find (alleged infringer's) use to be experimental, and thus not an infringement of (asserted patent(s)). If, however, you find that (alleged infringer's) use of the accused [product] [process] was in connection with a commercial purpose of (alleged infringer), then you should find that use not to have been experimental. In that case, the experimental use exception to infringement will not apply.

Authorities

Embrex, Inc. v. Serv. Eng'g Corp., 216 F.3d 1343, 1349 (Fed. Cir. 2000); *Warner-Lambert Co. v. Apotex Corp.*, 316 F.3d 1348 (Fed. Cir. 2003); *Allen Eng'g Corp. v. Bartell Indus., Inc.*, 299 F.3d 1336, 1352–55 (Fed. Cir. 2002); *Madey v. Duke Univ.*, 307 F.3d 1351, 1360–61 (Fed. Cir 2002); *Pitcairn v. United States*, 547 F.2d 1106, 1124–26 (Ct. Cl. 1976).

2.1.7 Infringement of Product-by-Process Claims

A product-by-process claim describes a product by the process by which it is made. For a product to infringe a product-by-process claim, it must be made by the same or an equivalent process to the one recited in the claim.

(Asserted claims) of (asserted patent(s)) are product-by-process claims. If you find that (patent holder) has proved by a preponderance of the evidence that (alleged infringer's) product is the same as, or equivalent to, the product described in the claims, and was made by the same process as the process recited in the claims, then you must find that (alleged infringer's) product infringes those claims.

Authorities

Abbott Labs. v. Sandoz, Inc., 566 F.3d 1282, 1293–95 (Fed. Cir. 2009) (en banc); *Vanguard Prod. Corp.* v. *Parker Hannifin Corp.,* 234 F.3d 1370, 1372–73 (Fed. Cir. 2000); *Exxon Chem. Patents, Inc.* v. *Lubrizol Corp.,* 64 F.3d 1553, 1557–58 (Fed. Cir. 1995); *Ex parte Alms,* No. 2009-2220, 2009 WL 819052, at *5 (B.P.A.I. Mar. 26, 2009); *Mentor Corp. v. Colopast, Inc.,* 998 F.2d 992, 997 (Fed. Cir. 1993); *Atl. Thermoplastics Co. v. Faytex Corp.,* 970 F.2d 834, 837 (Fed. Cir. 1992) reh'g en banc denied, 974 F.2d 1279 (Fed. Cir. 1992); *Aventis Pharm, Inc. v. Barr Labs, Inc.,* 335 F. Supp. 2d 558, 581–82 (D.N.J. 2004); *In re Thorpe,* 777 F.2d 695, 697 (Fed. Cir. 1985).

2.1.8 Infringement of Dependent Claims

(Asserted patent(s)) also contain(s) what are called dependent claims. A dependent claim includes each of the limitations of the independent claim to which it refers, plus additional elements described in the dependent claim itself.

If you find that independent claim(s) (asserted independent claim(s)) of (asserted patent(s)) has been infringed, you must separately determine whether dependent claim(s) (asserted dependent claim(s)) has also been infringed. If you find that the independent claims are not infringed, then you must also find that the dependent claims are not infringed.

Authorities

Jeneric/Pentron, Inc. v. Dillon Co., 205 F.3d 1377, 1383 (Fed. Cir. 2000); *In re Certain Gel-Filled Wrist Rests & Prods. Containing Same Comm'n Op.*, Inv. No. 337-TA-456, USITC Pub. 3573 (Jan. 1, 2003) (Final); *Finnigan Corp. v. Int'l Trade Comm'n,* 180 F.3d 1354, 1364 (Fed. Cir. 1999); *Cardinal Chem. Co. v. Morton Int'l, Inc.,* 508 U.S. 83 (1993); *Wahpeton Canvas Co. v. Frontier, Inc.,* 870 F.2d 1546, 1552–53 n.9 (Fed. Cir. 1989).

2.1.9 Open-Ended or "Comprising" Claims

[IF PREAMBLE USES "COMPRISING: The preamble to claim (asserted claim) uses the phrase [RECITE THE PREAMBLE "________ comprising"]. The word "comprising" means "including the following but not excluding others."

This means that (alleged infringer's) [product] [method] may include additional [components] [method steps] and still literally infringes the claim.]

[IF PREAMBLE USES "CONSISTING OF": The preamble to claim (asserted claim) uses the phrase [RECITE THE PREAMBLE "________ consisting of"]. The words "consisting of" mean "including the following and excluding others."

This means that if (alleged infringer's) [product] [method] includes additional [components] [method steps] beyond that described in the claims, you must find that (alleged infringer's) product does not literally infringe the claim.]

[IF PREAMBLE USES "CONSISTING ESSENTIALLY OF": The preamble to claim (asserted claim) uses the phrase [RECITE THE PREAMBLE

"________ consisting essentially of"]. The words "consisting essentially of" mean "including the following and possibly including unlisted [components] [method steps] that do not materially affect the invention."

This means that if (alleged infringer's) [product] [method] includes additional [components] [method steps] beyond that described in the claims and those [components] [steps] do materially affect the invention, you must find that (alleged infringer's) product does not literally infringe the claim.]

Authorities

Invitrogen Corp. v. Biocrest Mfg. LP, 327 F.3d 1364, 1368 (Fed. Cir. 2003); *AFG Indus. v. Cardinal IG Co.*, 239 F.3d 1239, 1244–45 (Fed. Cir. 2001); *Moleculon Research Corp. v. CBS, Inc.*, 793 F.2d 1261, 1271 (Fed. Cir. 1986); *AB Dick Co. v. Burroughs Corp.*, 713 F.2d 700, 703 (Fed. Cir. 1983).

2.1.10 Indirect Infringement

As I have told you, in addition to enforcing a patent against a direct infringer, a patent owner may also enforce the patent against indirect infringers. There are two types of indirect infringement: induced infringement and contributory infringement. "Induced infringement" is the act of encouraging or inducing others to infringe a patent. "Contributory infringement" is the act of contributing to others' infringement by, for example, supplying them with components used in the patented invention.

There can be no indirect infringement unless someone has directly infringed the patent. Thus, in order to prove that (alleged infringer) has induced another person to infringe or contributed to the infringement of another, (patent holder) must prove by a preponderance of the evidence that the other person has directly infringed at least one claim of the patent.

In this case, (patent holder) accuses (alleged infringer) of [inducing] [contributing to the] infringement of (asserted claim(s)) of (asserted patent(s)). (Patent holder) must prove by a preponderance of the evidence that (alleged infringer) has [induced] [contributed to the] infringement of at least one claim.

Note

Indirect infringement imposes patent infringement liability upon a third party who does not practice the claimed invention, but contributes to or aids in another's direct infringement. There are two types of *indirect* infringement—inducement and contributory infringement. 35 U.S.C. § 271(b) and (c). These two types of indirect infringement are addressed in Instructions II.B.1 and II.B.2, which should be read only if applicable to the case at issue.

2.1.11 Induced Patent Infringement

A person induces patent infringement if he or she purposefully causes, urges, or encourages another to infringe a patent. One must actively induce infringement. It cannot occur unintentionally. This is different from direct infringement, which, as I have told you, can occur unintentionally. To prove inducement, the patent owner must prove by a preponderance of the evidence that the accused inducer knew of the patent and encouraged or instructed another person to [use a product or perform a process] in a manner that infringed the patent. The patent owner must also prove by a preponderance of the evidence that the other person infringed the patent. However, it is not a defense to induced infringement that (alleged infringer) believed (asserted patent(s)) to be invalid.

(Patent holder) asserts that (alleged infringer) induced patent infringement. (Patent holder) must prove four things by a preponderance of the evidence:

First, (alleged infringer) encouraged or instructed another person how to [use a product or perform a process] in a manner that you, the jury, find infringes (asserted patent(s)).

Second, (alleged infringer) knew of (asserted patent(s)), or in the alternative, (alleged infringer) subjectively believed that there was a high probability that a patent covering the (accused product or process) existed, and (alleged infringer) took deliberate actions to avoid learning of the patent.

Third, (alleged infringer) knew that [its] [his] [her] encouragement or instructions would likely result in the other person doing that which you find to be an infringement of (asserted patent(s)).

Fourth, the other person infringed (asserted patent(s)).

If, and only if, you are persuaded of each of these four things may you find that (alleged infringer) induced patent infringement.

Note

35 U.S.C. § 271(b) provides that "[w]hoever actively induces infringement of a patent shall be liable as an infringer." Induced infringement "requires knowledge that the induced acts constitute patent *infringement*." *Global-Tech Appliances, Inc. v. SEB S.A.*, 563 U.S. 764, 766 (2011). An alleged infringer's good faith belief that the asserted patent is invalid is not a defense to induced infringement. *See Commil USA, LLC v. Cisco Sys., Inc.*, 575 U.S. 632 (2015). In light of *Commil*, an opinion of noninfringement may be used to defend against a claim of induced infringement, but an opinion of invalidity cannot. However, note that as to patents issued after September 16, 2012, and thus falling within the scope of the America Invents Act,

> [t]he failure of an infringer to obtain the advice of counsel with respect to any allegedly infringed patent, or the failure of the infringer to present such advice to the court or jury, may not be used to prove that the accused infringer willfully infringed the patent or that the infringer intended to induce infringement of the patent.

35 U.S.C. § 298. *See also Suprema, Inc. v. Int'l Trade Comm'n*, 626 Fed. App'x, 273, 282 n.2 (Fed. Cir. 2015). If failure to obtain a noninfringement opinion is at issue—and no motion *in limine* has been granted preventing a patent holder from seeking to prove willful blindness by failure to obtain opinion of counsel—an alleged infringer might seek to include the language of 35 U.S.C. § 298 as a penultimate paragraph in this instruction.

Induced infringement requires a complete act of direct infringement by a single actor or multiple actors found to have jointly infringed; a party "cannot be held liable for inducing infringement that never came to pass." *Limelight Networks, Inc. v. Akamai Techs., Inc.*, 572 U.S. 915, 923 (2014). Previous case law such as *Manville Sales Corp. v. Paramount Sys., Inc.*, 917 F.2d 544, 553 (Fed. Cir. 1990), recognized induced infringement liability where an alleged infringer "knew *or should have known*" that its encouragement or instructions would cause infringement; however, after *Global-Tech*, only actual knowledge or willful blindness to the fact of the infringement will meet the scienter requirement for induced infringement. (Emphasis added.) *See also Commil USA, LLC v. Cisco Sys., Inc.*, 720 F.3d 1361, 1366 (Fed. Cir. 2013), *vacated & remanded for other reasons*, 575 U.S. 632 ("[T]o the extent our prior case law allowed the finding of induced infringement based on recklessness or negligence, such case law is inconsistent with *Global-Tech* and no longer good law.").

Authorities

35 U.S.C. § 271(b); 35 U.S.C. § 298; *Commil USA, LLC v. Cisco Sys., Inc.*, 575 U.S. 632 (2015); *Commil USA, LLC v. Cisco Sys., Inc.*, 720 F.3d 1361, 1366 (Fed. Cir. 2013); *Suprema, Inc. v. Int'l Trade Comm'n*, 626 Fed. App'x 273 (Fed. Cir. 2015); *Global-Tech Appliances, Inc. v. SEB, S.A.*, 563 U.S. 754 (2011); *DSU Medical Corp. v. JMS Co.*, 471 F.3d 1293, 1304–06 (Fed. Cir. 2006) (en banc); *Metro-Goldwyn-Mayer Studios, Inc. v. Grokster, Ltd.*, 545 U.S. 913, 936 (2005); *Metabolite Labs., Inc. v. Lab. Corp. of Am. Holdings*, 370 F.3d 1354, 1365 (Fed. Cir. 2004); *Ferguson Beauregard/Logic Controls, Div. of Dover Res., Inc. v. Mega Sys., LLC*, 350 F.3d 1327, 1341–42 (Fed. Cir. 2003); *Manville Sales Corp. v. Paramount Sys., Inc.*, 917 F.2d 544, 553 (Fed. Cir. 1990); *Hewlett-Packard Co. v. Bausch & Lomb, Inc.*, 909 F.2d 1464, 1468–69 (Fed. Cir. 1990).

2.1.12 Contributory Infringement

Contributory infringement can occur when a person supplies a [component] [material] [apparatus] to another, and the person who receives the [component] [material] [apparatus] then infringes the patent. The [component] [material] [apparatus] must also have certain characteristics. First, the [component] [material] [apparatus] must be a material part of the invention. Second, the [component] [material] [apparatus] must be especially made or adapted for use in a manner that infringes the patent, and the supplier must know that the [component] [material] [apparatus] was especially made for that use. Third, the [component] [material] [apparatus] must not have a substantial use that does not infringe the patent. A [component] [material] [apparatus] that has a number of noninfringing uses is often referred to as a staple or commodity article. Providing such a staple or commodity article is not contributory infringement, even if the person to whom the article was supplied uses it in an infringing manner.

In this case, (patent holder) asserts that (alleged infringer's) selling or supplying of (relevant component, material, or apparatus) contributed to the infringement of (asserted claim(s)) of (asserted patent(s)). To establish that (alleged infringer) has contributorily infringed [that] [those] claim(s), (patent holder) must prove five things by a preponderance of the evidence:

First, (alleged infringer) knew of the patent, or, in the alternative, subjectively believed that there was a high probability that a patent covering the accused product or process existed, and (alleged infringer) took deliberate actions to avoid learning of the patent.

Second, [relevant component] [material] [apparatus] is a material component of the claimed invention and (alleged infringer) sold or supplied that [component] [material] [apparatus].

Third, (alleged infringer) knew that the intended use of the product would infringe the patent.

Fourth, the [component] [material] [apparatus] has no substantial noninfringing use.

Fifth, the [component] [material] [apparatus] was actually used by someone other than (alleged infringer) in a manner that you find infringes the patent.

If, and only if, you are persuaded of each of these five things may you find that (alleged infringer) contributed to infringement.

Note

35 U.S.C. § 271(c) provides the following:

> Whoever offers to sell or sells within the United States or imports into the United States a component of a patented machine, manufacture, combination or composition, or a material or apparatus for use in practicing a patented process, constituting a material part of

> the invention, knowing the same to be especially made or especially adapted for use in an infringement of such patent, and not a staple article or commodity of commerce suitable for substantial noninfringing use, shall be liable as a contributory infringer.

Authorities

35 U.S.C. § 271(c); *Commil USA, LLC v. Cisco Sys., Inc.*, 135 S. Ct. 1920, 1926 (2015) ("Like induced infringement, contributory infringement requires knowledge of the patent in suit and knowledge of patent infringement."); *Toshiba Corp. v. Imation Corp.*, 681 F.3d 1358, 1362 (Fed. Cir. 2012); *In re Bill of Lading Transm. & Process. Sys. Patent Litig.*, 681 F.3d 1323, 1337–38 (2012); *Spansion, Inc. v. Int'l Trade Comm'n*, 629 F.3d 1331, 1353 (Fed. Cir. 2010); *Fujitsu Ltd. v. Netgear, Inc.*, 620 F.3d 1321 (Fed. Cir. 2010); *i4i Ltd. P'ship v. Microsoft Corp.*, 598 F.3d 831, 848–49 (Fed. Cir. 2010) (finding no reversible error in a contributory infringement instruction that used the term "component" for a patented process rather than "material or apparatus" when the parties' arguments did not turn on whether an invention was a "component" or a "material or apparatus"); *Aro Mfg. Co. v. Convertible Top Replacement Co.*, 377 U.S. 476, 485–90 (1964).

2.2 Willful Infringement

(Patent holder) also contends that (alleged infringer) has willfully infringed (asserted patent(s)) claims. If you find, on the basis of the evidence and the law as I have explained it, that (alleged infringer) directly or indirectly infringed at least one claim of (asserted patent(s)), you must then decide whether (alleged infringer's) infringement was willful. To establish willful infringement, (patent holder) must prove by a preponderance of the evidence that (alleged infringer) acted with reckless disregard of at least one claim of the patent.

While there is no set test in determining whether infringement is willful, you should consider the (alleged infringer's) knowledge at the time of infringement, and you may consider the following factors:

(1) whether (alleged infringer) acted in a manner consistent with the standards of commerce for [its] [his] [her] industry;
(2) whether (alleged infringer) intentionally copied the claimed invention of (asserted patent(s)) or a product covered by (asserted patent(s));
(3) whether (alleged infringer) made a good-faith effort to avoid infringing (asserted patent(s)), for example, by attempting to design around the patent;
(4) whether (alleged infringer) held a reasonable belief that (asserted patent(s)) [was] [were] not infringed, invalid, or unenforceable; and
(5) whether (alleged infringer) tried to cover up [its] [his] [her] infringement[; and]

[Give this instruction only if (alleged infringer) relies upon an opinion of counsel as a defense to an allegation of willful infringement.]:

(6) whether (alleged infringer) relied on an opinion of counsel that (asserted patent(s)) [was] [were] not infringed, invalid, or unenforceable.

(Alleged infringer) argues [it] [he] [she] did not act recklessly because [it] [he] [she] relied on a legal opinion that advised (alleged infringer) (1) that the [product] [method] did not infringe (asserted patent(s)), or (2) that the (asserted patent(s)) was invalid [or unenforceable]. You must evaluate whether the opinion was sufficiently competent that reliance on its conclusion was reasonable. In determining the competence of the opinion, you may consider a number of factors, including, but not limited to:

(1) whether the opinion was written or oral;
(2) whether the opinion was rendered by a patent attorney;
(3) whether the opinion was rendered by independent outside counsel; and
(4) whether the opinion was thorough, or merely conclusory in nature.

Note

In 2007, the Federal Circuit overturned the existing "duty of due care" standard set forth in *Underwater Devices, Inc. v. Morrison-Knudsen, Co.*,

717 F.2d 1380, 1389 (Fed. Cir. 1983), finding that it was "more akin to negligence" than willful misconduct. *In re Seagate Tech., LLC,* 497 F.3d 1360, 1371 (Fed. Cir. 2007) (en banc). Relying on Supreme Court precedent requiring a showing of recklessness before civil punitive damages are allowed, the Circuit Court held that proof of willfulness now required "at least a showing of objective recklessness." *Id.* In implementing the new standard, the Federal Circuit created a two-part test for establishing willful infringement. The first, and threshold, prong was an objective test under which the patentee must prove that "the infringer acted despite an objectively high likelihood that its actions constituted infringement of a valid patent." *Seagate,* 497 F.3d at 1371. The second prong was a subjective test requiring a showing that the risk of infringement "was either known or so obvious that it should have been known to the accused infringer." *Id.* The two-part *Seagate* test has since been abrogated by *Halo Electronics, Inc. v. Pulse Electronics, Inc.*, 136 S. Ct. 1923 (2016), and "[u]nder *Halo*, the concept of 'willfulness' requires a jury to find no more than deliberate or intentional infringement." *Eko Brands, LLC v. Adrian Rivera Maynez Enter., Inc.*, 946 F.3d 1367, 1378 (Fed. Cir. 2020).

Accused infringers often rely on opinions of counsel as evidence of their good faith. But drawing an adverse inference is inappropriate in situations where the infringer had either not received an opinion or had received one but had declined to rely on it in the litigation. *Knorr-Bremse*, 383 F.3d at 1342. The Federal Circuit further expanded on this in *Seagate*, holding that the abrogation of the "duty of due care" standard necessarily led to the conclusion that an alleged infringer does not have an affirmative duty to obtain an opinion of counsel. *Seagate*, 497 F.3d at 1371. In cases where infringers choose to rely on opinions of counsel as evidence of their good faith, the Federal Circuit considers a number of factors to determine whether an opinion of counsel was competent and, therefore, could provide a sufficient basis for the accused infringer's good-faith belief:

(1) whether the opinion written or oral [*Minnesota Mining & Mfg. v. Johnson & Johnson Orthopedics, Inc.*, 976 F.2d 1559, 1580 (Fed. Cir. 1992) (noting that the Federal Circuit does not favor oral opinions)];

(2) whether a patent attorney gave the opinion [*Underwater Devices, Inc. v. Morrison-Knudsen, Co.*, 717 F.2d 1380, 1390 (Fed. Cir. 1983)];
(3) whether in-house or outside counsel gave the opinion [*Id.*]; and
(4) whether the opinion was conclusory in nature or provided a thorough analysis of the relevant issues [*Read Corp. v. Portee, Inc.*, 970 F.2d 816, 829–30 (Fed. Cir. 1992)].

The most important factor in determining whether the accused infringer's reliance on counsel's advice was sufficient is the presence or absence of objective evidence that would have alerted the infringer that the opinion was untrustworthy. *See, e.g.*, *Read*, 970 F.2d at 829 ("A written opinion may be incompetent on its face by reason of its containing merely conclusory statements without discussion of facts or obviously presenting only a superficial or off-the-cuff analysis.").

Authorities

35 U.S.C. § 284; *Eko Brands, LLC v. Adrian Rivera Maynez Enter., Inc.*, 946 F.3d 1367, 1378 (Fed. Cir. 2020) (explaining the Halo test); *Halo Elec., Inc. v. Pulse Elec., Inc.*, 136 S. Ct. 1923 (2016) (abrogating Seagate); *Carnegie Mellon Univ. v. Marvell Tech. Grp., Ltd.*, 807 F.3d 1283 (Fed. Cir. 2015) (explaining the standards of review and noting that there is no requirement for an alleged infringer to have a reasonable defense prior to litigation); *SSL Servs., LLC v. Citrix Sys., Inc.*, 769 F.3d 1073, 1090 (Fed. Cir. 2014) (stating that the second Seagate prong is a factual matter subject to review for substantial evidence); *Halo Elec., Inc. v. Pulse Elec., Inc.*, 769 F.3d 1371 (Fed. Cir. 2014) (noting that the first Seagate prong is a matter of law subject to de novo review); *Bard Peripheral Vascular, Inc. v. W.L. Gore & Assoc., Inc.*, 682 F.3d 1003 (Fed. Cir. 2012) (explaining the standards of review and discussing how the objective reasonableness of a defense does not require that the infringer had the defense in mind before the litigation); *i4i Ltd. P'ship v. Microsoft Corp.*, 598 F.3d 831 (Fed. Cir. 2010) aff'd, 564 U.S. 91 (2011) (discussing enhanced damages); *In re Seagate Tech., LLC*, 497 F.3d 1360 (Fed. Cir. 2007) (stating the standard for finding willfulness); *Safeco Ins. Co. of Am. v. Burr*, 551 U.S. 47 (2007) (standard civil usage of "willful" reaches both knowing violations and those done in

"reckless disregard"); *Liquid Dynamics Corp. v. Vaughan Co.*, 449 F.3d 1209 (Fed. Cir. 2006) (competency of opinion of counsel); *Knorr-Bremse Systeme Fuer Nutzfahrzeuge GmbH v. Dana Corp.*, 383 F.3d 1337 (Fed. Cir. 2004) (opinion of counsel defense); *Graco, Inc. v. Binks Mfg. Co.*, 60 F.3d 785 (Fed. Cir. 1995) (jury to consider totality of the circumstances); *Minnesota Mining & Mfg. v. Johnson & Johnson Orthopedics, Inc.*, 976 F.2d 1559 (Fed. Cir. 1992) (competency of opinion of counsel); *Read Corp. v. Portee, Inc.*, 970 F.2d 816 (Fed. Cir. 1992) (superseded on other grounds as recognized in *Hoechst Celanese Corp. v. BP Chems. Ltd.*, 78 F.3d 1575 (Fed. Cir. 1996)) (enhanced damages factors and competency of opinion of counsel); *Underwater Devices, Inc. v. Morrison-Knudsen, Co.*, 717 F.2d 1380 (Fed. Cir. 1983) (competency of opinion of counsel).

2.3 Design Patents; Infringement Generally

I will now instruct you as to the rules you must follow when deciding whether (the patent holder) has proven that (alleged infringer) has directly infringed (the patent holder's) design patent(s).

[As with utility patents,] Patent law gives the owner of a valid design patent the right to exclude others from importing, making, using, offering to sell, or selling the patented designs within the United States during the term of the patent. Any person or company that has engaged in any of those acts without the design patent owner's permission infringes the patent.

In deciding whether a sale has taken place "within the United States," you may find the following guidelines helpful to your analysis: The location of the sale depends on many factors, and you may find that the sale occurred in several places. A sale occurs wherever the "essential activities" of the sale take place. The essential activities include, for example, negotiating the contract and performing obligations under the contract.

[FOR MULTIPLE ALLEGATIONS OF DESIGN PATENT INFRINGEMENT: (Patent holder) bears the burden of proving by a preponderance of the evidence that each of (alleged infringer's) products infringes each separate patent. Therefore, you, the jury, must determine infringement for each patent separately, considering each individual product separately.]

Authorities

35 U.S.C. § 171; 35 U.S.C. §§ 271–73; *L.A. Gear, Inc. v. Thom McAn Shoe Co.*, 988 F.2d 1117, 1122 (Fed. Cir. 1993); *Crocs, Inc. v. Int'l Trade Comm'n*, 598 F.3d 1294, 1302 (Fed. Cir. 2010); *Smith v. Whitman Saddle Co*, 148 U.S. 674, 677–78 (1893).

2.3.1 Design Patents; Direct Infringement

To determine direct infringement of a design patent, you must compare the overall appearances of the accused design and the claimed design. Remember that the claimed design is limited to matter depicted in solid lines in the drawing(s)—any matter depicted in dashed lines is not protected by the design patent.

If you find by a preponderance of the evidence that the overall appearance of (alleged infringer's) design is substantially the same as the overall appearance of (patent holder's) claimed design patent, and that the accused design was made, used, sold, offered for sale, or imported within the United States, you must find that the accused design infringed the claimed design.

Two designs are substantially the same if, in the eye of an ordinary observer, giving such attention as a purchaser usually gives, the resemblance between the two designs is such as to deceive such an observer, inducing him to purchase one thinking it to be the other. You do not need, however, to find that any purchasers actually were deceived or confused by the appearance of the accused products. You should consider any perceived similarities or differences between the patented and accused designs. Minor differences should not prevent a finding of infringement.

This determination of whether two designs are substantially the same will benefit from comparing the two designs with prior art. You must familiarize yourself with the prior art admitted at trial in making your determination of whether there has been direct infringement.

You may find the following guidelines helpful to your analysis:

(1) The placement and ornamentation of a logo may alter the overall design. However, the use of a mark or logo to identify the source of an otherwise infringing design will not avoid infringement.

(2) When the claimed design is visually close to prior art designs, small differences between the accused design and the claimed design may be important in analyzing whether the overall appearances of the accused and claimed designs are substantially the same.
(3) If the accused design includes a feature of the claimed design that departs conspicuously from the prior art, you may find that feature is important in analyzing whether the overall appearance of the accused and claimed designs are substantially the same.
(4) If the accused design is visually closer to the claimed design than it is to the closest prior art, you may find this comparison important in analyzing whether the overall appearances of the accused and claimed designs are substantially the same.
(5) You should not consider the size of the accused products if the asserted design patent does not specify the size of the design.

While these guidelines may be helpful, the test for infringement is whether the overall appearances of the accused design and the claimed design are substantially the same.

Whether (alleged infringer) knew its products infringed or even knew of (patent holder's) design patents does not matter in determining infringement.

Authorities

35 U.S.C. §§ 271–73; *Crocs, Inc. v. Int'l Trade Comm'n*, 598 F.3d 1294, 1302 (Fed. Cir. 2010); *Columbia Sportswear N. Am., Inc. v. Seirus Innovative Accessories, Inc.*, 942 F.3d 1119, 1129–30 (Fed. Cir. 2019); *Lanard Toys Ltd. v. Dolgencorp LLC*, 958 F.3d 1337, 1341 (Fed. Cir. 2020); *Egyptian Goddess, Inc. v. Swisa, Inc.*, 543 F.3d 665, 675–76 (Fed. Cir. 2008); *Lawman Armor Corp. v. Winner Int'l, LLC*, 437 F.3d 1383, 1385–86 (Fed. Cir. 2006).

2.3.2 Design Patent; Product Comparisons

In deciding the issue of infringement, you must compare (alleged infringer's) accused products to the design patents. In addition, you have heard evidence about certain products and models produced by (patent holder). If you determine that any of (patent holder's) products or models are substantially the same as (patent holder's) patent design, and that the product or model has no significant distinctions with the design, you may compare the product or model directly to the accused products. This may facilitate your determination of whether the accused products infringe (patent holder's) patented design. If you determine that a particular (patent holder) product or model does not embody a patented design, you may not compare it to the accused products.

Authorities

OddzOn Prod., Inc. v. Just Toys, Inc., 122 F.3d 1396, 1404–05 (Fed. Cir. 1997); *Egyptian Goddess, Inc. v. Swisa, Inc.*, 543 F.3d 665, 675–76 (Fed. Cir. 2008); *Crocs, Inc. v. Int'l Trade Comm'n*, 598 F.3d 1294, 1303–04 (Fed. Cir. 2010); *Richardson v. Stanley Works, Inc.*, 597 F.3d 1288, 1295–96 (Fed. Cir. 2010).

Chapter Three

INVALIDITY

3.1 Overview

As I stated previously, (alleged infringer) contends that the asserted claims are invalid. I will now explain to you each of the grounds for invalidity that were presented by (alleged infringer) at trial. A party must meet its burden of proof on only one of these grounds in order to invalidate a claim.

3.1.1 Utility Patents; Overview

For a patent to be valid, the invention claimed in the patent must be new, useful, and nonobvious. The terms "new," "useful," and "nonobvious" have special meanings under the patent laws that I will explain to you as I discuss (alleged infringer's) grounds for asserting invalidity.

3.1.2 Design Patents; Overview

For a design patent to be valid, the claimed design must be new, ornamental, and nonobvious. The terms "new," "ornamental," and "nonobvious" have special meanings under the patent laws that I will explain to you as I discuss (alleged infringer's) grounds for asserting invalidity.

3.1.3 Burden of Proof and Presumption of Validity [Design/Utility Patent]

Although (asserted patent(s)) [was] [were] granted by the Patent and Trademark Office, it is your job to determine whether (alleged infringer) has proven, by clear and convincing evidence, that the legal requirements for patentability were not met.

[IF ALLEGED INFRINGER RELIED ON PRIOR ART NOT CITED ON PATENT(S):] During this case, (alleged infringer) has submitted prior art that was not considered by the USPTO during the prosecution of the (asserted patent(s)). (Alleged infringer) contends that such prior art invalidates certain claims of the (asserted patent(s)). In deciding the issue of invalidity, you may take into account the fact that the prior art was not considered by the USPTO when it issued (asserted patent(s)). Prior art that differs from the prior art considered by the USPTO may carry more weight than the prior art that was considered and may make (alleged infringer's) burden of showing by clear and convincing evidence that a patent claim is invalid easier to meet.

I will now explain to you (alleged infringer's) grounds for invalidity in detail. In making your determination regarding invalidity, you should consider each claim of the (asserted patent(s)) separately.

3.1.4 Prior Art for Claims Having a Priority Date *before* March 16, 2013 [Design/Utility Patent]

As I stated previously, under the patent laws, an inventor is granted a patent only if the [invention] [design] claimed in the patent is new and not obvious in light of what came before. That which came before is referred to as the "prior art." (Alleged infringer) must prove that these items are prior art. To do so, (alleged infringer) must prove that the items fall within one or more of the different categories of prior art recognized by the patent laws. These categories include:

First, any [product] [method] that was publicly known or used in the United States by someone other than the inventor before the inventor made the [invention] [claimed design].

Second, any [product] [method] that was in public use or on sale in the United States more than one year before the application for the patent was filed.

Third, any patent or printed publication that was publicly available before the inventor made the [invention] [claimed design], or more than one year before the application for the patent was filed.

Fourth, any [product] [method] that was [invented] [made] by another person in this country before the inventor made the invention, if the other person did not abandon, suppress, or conceal his or her prior invention.

[IF MULTIPLE PATENTS WITH DIFFERENT PRIORITY DATES:]

[The] [One or more of the] asserted patents were filed on different dates. Therefore, you must separately decide whether the asserted claims are invalid in view of the prior art and the ordinary skill in the art as it existed as of the dates of invention of each of the patents in question.]

In this case, (alleged infringer) contends that the following items are prior art:

[Identify prior art admitted into evidence.]

3.1.5 Prior Art for Claims Having a Priority Date *after* March 16, 2013 [Design/Utility Patent]

As I stated previously, under the patent laws, an inventor is granted a patent only if the invention claimed in the patent is new and not obvious in light of what came before. That which came before is referred to as the "prior art." (Alleged infringer) must prove that these items are prior art. To do so, (alleged infringer) must prove that the items fall within one or more of the different categories of prior art recognized by the patent laws. These categories include:

First, prior art includes any claimed invention that was patented, described in a printed publication, or in public use, on sale, or otherwise available to the public anywhere in the world before (effective filing date).

There are two exceptions to this category of prior art. A disclosure under this category is not considered prior art if it was made one year or less before (effective filing date) and was either (1) made by (inventor of asserted patent(s)) or by someone else who obtained the subject matter from the inventor, or (2) the subject matter disclosed had previously been publicly disclosed by (inventor of asserted patent(s)) or someone who obtained the subject matter from [him] [her].

Second, prior art includes any claimed invention that was described in a patent, or in an application for patent published or deemed published, in which the patent or application names another inventor and was filed before (effective filing date).

There are several exceptions to this category of prior art. A disclosure under this category is not prior art to the claims if either (1) the subject matter disclosed was obtained directly or indirectly from (inventor of asserted patent(s)); (2) the subject matter disclosed had, before (effective filing date), been publicly disclosed by (inventor of asserted patent(s)) or someone who obtained the subject matter from [him] [her]; or (3) the subject matter disclosed and the claimed invention were owned by the same person no later than (effective filing date).

In this case, (alleged infringer) contends that the following items are prior art:

[Identify prior art admitted into evidence.]

3.1.6 Level of Ordinary Skill

3.1.6.1 Level of Ordinary Skill for Claims Having a Priority Date *before* March 16, 2013

The question of invalidity of a patent claim is determined from the perspective of a person of ordinary skill in the art in the field of the asserted invention as of (date of invention). You must determine the level of ordinary skill in the field of the invention. The higher the level of ordinary skill, the easier it may be to establish that an invention would have been obvious. Persons having a greater level of education, training, or experience in the field will more readily appreciate technical details that may be more challenging for persons having a lower level of skill. On the other hand, persons having a lower level of skill may not perceive as obvious technical details that would be apparent to persons having greater skill. To determine the obviousness of the invention you will be asked to determine what the ordinary level of skill was in the field of the invention.

3.1.6.2 Level of Ordinary Skill for Claims Having a Priority Date *after* March 16, 2013

The question of invalidity of a patent claim is determined from the perspective of a person of ordinary skill in the art in the field of the asserted invention as of (effective filing date). You must determine the level of ordinary skill in the field of the invention. The higher the level of ordinary skill, the easier it may be to establish that an invention would have been obvious. Persons having a greater level of education, training, or experience in the field will more readily appreciate technical details that may be more challenging for persons having a lower level of skill. On the other hand, persons having a lower level of skill may not perceive as obvious technical details that would be apparent to persons having greater skill. To determine the obviousness of the invention you will be asked to determine what the ordinary level of skill was in the field of the invention.

3.2 Anticipation; Design Patents

A design patent claim is invalid if the claimed invention is not new. For the claim to be invalid because it is not new, the claimed design must be substantially similar to one that has been described in a single prior art reference that predates the claimed invention. If a patent claim is not new, then we say it is "anticipated" by a prior art reference.

The same standard of "substantial similarity" or "substantially the same" that applies to infringement also applies to anticipation. That is, the single prior art reference and the claimed design patent are substantially the same if, in the eye of the ordinary observer, giving such attention as a purchaser usually gives, the resemblance between the two designs is such as to deceive such an observer, inducing him to purchase one supposing it to be the other.

You should consider any perceived similarities or differences between the claimed design and prior art reference. Minor differences should not prevent a finding of anticipation.

Authorities

Door-Master Corp. v. Yorktowne, Inc., 256 F.3d 1308, 1312–14 (Fed. Cir. 2001); *OddzOn Prods., Inc. v. Just Toys, Inc.*, 122 F.3d 1396, 1405 (Fed. Cir. 1997); *Hafco Foundry & Mach. Co., Inc. v. GMS Mine Repair & Maint., Inc.*, 953 F.3d 745, 751 (Fed. Cir. 2020); *Egyptian Goddess, Inc. v. Swisa, Inc.*, 543 F.3d 665 (Fed. Cir. 2008).

3.3 Anticipation; Utility Patents

A patent claim is invalid if the claimed invention is not new. For the claim to be invalid because it is not new, all of its limitations must have existed in a single device or method that predates the claimed invention or must have been described in a single previous prior art reference that predates the claimed invention. As I have discussed, in patent law, these previous devices, methods, publications, or patents are called "prior art references." If a patent claim is not new, then we say it is "anticipated" by a prior art reference.

In determining whether the invention is anticipated, you must determine the scope and content of the prior art at the time the invention was made. You must decide whether the specific reference(s) relied upon by (alleged infringer) in this case [is] [are] prior art to the invention described in the asserted claim(s). Once you decide whether or not specific reference(s) [is] [are] prior art, you must also decide what [that] [those] reference(s) would have disclosed or taught to one having ordinary skill in the field of technology of the patent at the time the invention was made.

The description in the prior art reference does not have to use the same words as the claim, but all the requirements of the claim must be present, either stated expressly or necessarily implied, so that someone of ordinary skill in the field of technology of the patent looking at the one reference would be able to make and use the claimed invention. The prior art reference(s) must disclose each end every element of the claimed invention so that a person of ordinary skill in the art could take its teachings together with his or her own knowledge of the art and be able to make and use the claimed invention.

(Alleged infringer) contends that claims (asserted claims) of the (asserted patent(s)) are invalid because the claimed invention is not new. If a patent claim is not new, you must find the claim invalid.

3.3.1 Prior Public Knowledge

3.3.1.1 For Claims with an Effective Filing Date *before* March 16, 2013

(Alleged infringer) contends that (challenged claim(s)) of (patent(s)) are invalid as anticipated because the invention defined in [that claim] [those claims] was publicly known by others in the United States before [it was] [they were] invented. A patent claim is invalid if the invention defined in that claim was available to the public before it was invented by (named inventor).

3.3.1.2 For Claims with an Effective Filing Date *after* March 16, 2013

(Alleged infringer) contends that (challenged claim(s)) of (patent(s)) are invalid as anticipated because the invention defined in [that claim] [those claims] was available to the public before the effective filing date of the claimed invention(s). A patent claim is invalid if the invention defined in that claim was available to the public before the effective filing date of the claimed invention.

Authorities

35 U.S.C. § 102(a) (pre-AIA); 35 U.S.C. § 102(a)(1) (AIA); *Carella v. Starlight Archery & Pro Line Co.*, 804 F.2d 135 (Fed. Cir. 1986); *Woodland Trust v. Flowertree Nursery, Inc.*, 148 F.3d 1368, 1370 (Fed. Cir. 1998); *Minn. Mining & Mfg. Co. v. Chemque, Inc.*, 303 F.3d 1294, 1301, 1306 (Fed. Cir. 2002).

3.3.2 Prior Public Use

3.3.2.1 For Claims with an Effective Filing Date *before* March 16, 2013

(Alleged infringer) contends that (challenged claim(s)) of (patent(s)) are invalid as anticipated because the invention defined in [that claim] [those claims] [was publicly used by others in the United States before it was invented by (named inventor(s))] [was publicly used in the United States more than one year before (named inventor(s)) filed [his] [her] [their] patent application on (effective filing date)].

A patent claim is invalid if more than one year before (effective filing date) an embodiment of the claimed invention was both (1) in public use, and (2) ready for patenting.

An invention was in public use if the claimed invention was accessible to the public or commercially exploited. Factors relevant to determining whether a use was public include: (1) the nature of the activity that occurred in public, (2) public access to the use, (3) confidentiality obligations imposed upon observers, (4) commercial exploitation, and (5) the circumstances surrounding any testing and experimentation.

An invention was publicly used if it was used by the inventor or by a person who was not under any limitation, restriction, or obligation of secrecy to the inventor. The absence of affirmative steps to conceal the use of the invention is evidence of a public use. But secret use by a third party is not public unless members of the public or employees of the third party had access to the invention.

To be a public use, the invention also must have been ready for patenting at the time of the alleged public use. An invention is ready for patenting either when it is reduced to practice or when the inventor has prepared drawings or other descriptions of the invention sufficient to allow a person of ordinary skill in the art to make or use the invention. An invention is reduced to practice when it has been: (1) constructed or performed within the scope of the patent claims, and (2) determined that it works for its intended purpose.

3.3.2.2 For Claims with an Effective Filing Date *after* March 16, 2013

(Alleged infringer) contends that (challenged claim(s)) of (patent(s)) are invalid as anticipated because the invention defined in [that claim] [those claims] was publicly used anywhere in the world before (effective filing date).

A patent claim is invalid if before the effective filing date of the claimed invention, an embodiment of the claimed invention was both (1) in public use, and (2) ready for patenting.

An invention was in public use if the claimed invention was accessible to the public or commercially exploited anywhere in the world. Factors relevant to determining whether a use was public include: (1) the nature of the activity that occurred in public, (2) public access to the use, (3) confidentiality obligations imposed upon observers, (4) commercial exploitation, and (5) the circumstances surrounding testing and experimentation. An invention was publicly used if it was used by the inventor or by a person who was not under any limitation, restriction, or obligation of secrecy to the inventor. The absence of affirmative steps to conceal the use of the invention is evidence of a public use. But secret use by a third party is not public unless members of the public or employees of the third party have access to the invention.

To be a public use, the invention also must have been ready for patenting at the time of the alleged public use. An invention is ready for patenting either when it is reduced to practice or when the inventor has prepared drawings or other descriptions of the invention sufficient to allow a person of ordinary skill in the art to make or use the invention. An invention is reduced to practice when it has been: (1) constructed or performed within the scope of the patent claims, and (2) determined that it works for its intended purpose.

Authorities

35 U.S.C. § 102(a), (b) (pre-AIA); 35 U.S.C. § 102(a)(1) (AIA); *W.L. Gore & Assoc. v. Garlock, Inc.*, 721 F.2d 1540, 1549–50 (Fed. Cir. 1983); *Abbott Labs. v. Geneva Pharms., Inc.*, 182 F.3d 1315, 1319 (Fed. Cir.

1999); *SmithKline Beecham Corp. v. Apotex Corp.*, 365 F.3d 1306, 1316–20 (Fed. Cir. 2004); *Invitrogen Corp. v. Biocrest Mfg., L.P.*, 424 F.3d 1374, 1379–82 (Fed. Cir. 2005); *Clock Spring, L.P. v. Wrapmaster, Inc.*, 560 F.3d 1317, 1325–27 (Fed. Cir. 2009).

3.3.3 On-Sale Bar

3.3.3.1 For Claims with an Effective Filing Date *before* March 16, 2013

(Alleged infringer) contends that (challenged claim(s)) of (patent(s)) are invalid as anticipated because the invention defined in [that claim] [those claims] was on sale in the United States more than one year before (named inventor(s)) filed [his] [her] [their] patent application on (effective filing date).

A patent claim is invalid if more than one year before the filing date of the patent an embodiment of the claimed invention was both subject to commercial offer for sale in the United States and ready for patenting.

A commercial "offer for sale" was made if another party could make a binding contract by simply accepting the offer. An invention was subject to an "offer for sale" if the claimed invention was embodied in an item that was actually sold or offered for sale. It is not required that a sale was actually made, as long as it was offered for sale.

The invention also must have been "ready for patenting" more than one year before the filing date of the patent. An invention is ready for patenting either when it is reduced to practice or when the inventor has prepared drawings or other descriptions of the invention that were sufficiently specific to enable a person of ordinary skill in the field to practice the invention. An invention is reduced to practice when it has been (1) constructed or performed within the scope of the patent claims, and (2) determined that it works for its intended purpose.

3.3.3.2 For Claims with an Effective Filing Date *after* March 16, 2013

(Alleged infringer) contends that (challenged claim(s)) of (patent(s)) are invalid as anticipated because the invention defined in [that claim] [those claims] was on sale before (named inventor(s)) filed [his] [her] [their] patent application on (effective filing date).

A patent claim is invalid if it was on sale before the effective filing date of the claimed invention. A commercial "offer for sale" was made if another party could make a binding contract by simply accepting the offer. An invention was subject to an "offer for sale" if the claimed invention was embodied in an item that was actually sold or offered for sale. It is not required that a sale was actually made.

A commercial "offer for sale" was made by the inventor if the claimed invention was embodied in an item that was actually sold or offered for sale, and the invention was "ready for patenting" before the effective filing date of the claimed invention. This applies even if the invention is sold to a third party who is contractually required to keep the invention confidential. An invention is ready for patenting either when it is reduced to practice or when the inventor has prepared drawings or other descriptions of the invention that was sufficiently specific to enable a person of ordinary skill in the art to practice the invention. An invention is reduced to practice when it has been (1) constructed or performed within the scope of the patent claims, and (2) determined that it works for its intended purpose.

Authorities

35 U.S.C. § 102(b) (pre-AIA); 35 U.S.C. § 102(a)(1) (AIA); *Elizabeth v. Pavement Co.*, 97 U.S. 126, 134–35 (1877); *Pfaff v. Wells Elec. Inc.*, 525 U.S. 55 (1998); *Buildex, Inc. v. Kason Indus., Inc.*, 849 F.2d 1461, 1463 (Fed. Cir. 1988); *Abbott Labs. v. Geneva Pharms., Inc.*, 182 F.3d 1315, 1319 (Fed. Cir. 1999); *EZ Dock, Inc. v. Schafer Sys.*, 276 F.3d 1347, 1357 (Fed. Cir. 2002) (Linn, J., concurring); *Cont'l Plastic Containers v. Owens Brockway Plastic Prods., Inc.*, 141 F.3d 1073, 1079 (Fed. Cir. 1998); *Clock Spring, L.P. v. Wrapmaster, Inc.*, 560 F.3d 1317, 1325–27 (Fed. Cir. 2009); *Helsinn Healthcare S.A. v. Teva Pharms.*, 139 S. Ct. 628, 633–34 (2019).

3.3.4 Prior Invention [Only Applies to Claims with an Effective Filing Date *before* March 16, 2013]

(Alleged infringer) contends that (challenged claim(s)) of (patent(s)) are invalid as anticipated because the invention defined in [that claim] [those claims] was invented by another person (name of third party) before (named inventor(s)) invented [his] [her] [their] invention.

If a device or process has been previously invented, then it is not new. An invention made by another person before (the named inventor(s)) conceived of [his] [her] [their] invention is prior art as long as the prior inventor did not abandon, suppress, or conceal the invention.

Authorities

35 U.S.C. § 102(a), (g) (pre-AIA); *Apotex U.S.A., Inc. v. Merck & Co.*, 254 F.3d 1031, 1035 (Fed. Cir. 2001); *Teva Pharm. Indus. v. AstraZeneca Pharm.*, 661 F.3d 1378 (Fed. Cir. 2011).

3.3.5 Prior Patent

3.3.5.1 For Claims with an Effective Filing Date *before* March 16, 2013

(Alleged infringer) contends that (challenged claim(s)) of (patent(s)) are invalid as anticipated because the invention defined in [that claim] [those claims] was patented by (third party) [before it was invented by (named inventor(s))] [more than one year before (named inventor(s)) filed [his] [her] [their] patent application on (U.S. filing date)].

A patent claim is invalid if the invention defined by that claim was patented in the United States or a foreign country [before it was invented by (the patentee)] [more than one year before (the patentee) filed his United States patent application].

3.3.5.2 For Claims with an Effective Filing Date *after* March 16, 2013

(Alleged infringer) contends that (challenged claim(s)) of (patent(s)) are invalid as anticipated because the invention defined in [that claim] [those claims] was patented by (third party) before the effective filing date of the claimed invention.

A patent claim is invalid if the invention defined by that claim was patented in the United States or a foreign country before the effective filing date of the claimed invention.

Authorities

35 U.S.C. § 102(a), (b) (pre-AIA); 35 U.S.C. § 102(a)(1), § 102(b)(1) (AIA); *Advanced Display Sys., Inc. v. Kent State Univ.*, 212 F.3d 1272, 1277–83 (Fed. Cir. 2000).

3.3.6 Prior Patent Application

3.3.6.1 For Claims with an Effective Filing Date *before* March 16, 2013

(Alleged infringer) contends that (challenged claim(s)) of (patent(s)) are invalid as anticipated because the invention defined in [that claim] [those claims] was described in United States [published patent application] [patent] (published application number) (anticipating patent number), and because [the published patent application (published application number)] [application for the (anticipating patent number) patent] was filed before (named inventor(s)) made [his] [her] [their] invention.

(Challenged claim(s)) of (challenged patent(s)) are invalid if the invention defined by [that claim] [those claims] was described in a [published United States patent application] [United States patent] filed by another person before the invention was made by (named inventor(s)).

3.3.6.2 For Claims with an Effective Filing Date *after* March 16, 2013

(Alleged infringer) contends that (challenged claim(s)) of (patent(s)) are invalid as anticipated because the invention defined in [that claim] [those claims] was described in United States [published patent application] [patent] (published application number) (anticipating patent number), and because [the published patent application (published application number)] [application for the (anticipating patent number) patent] was filed before the effective filing date of the claimed invention.

(Challenged claim(s)) of (challenged patent(s)) are invalid if the invention defined by [that claim] [those claims] was described in a published patent application filed by another person before the effective filing date of the claimed invention.

Authorities

35 U.S.C. §102(e)(1), (2) (pre-AIA); 35 U.S.C. §102(a)(2), (b)(2), (c), (d) (AIA); *In re Giacomini*, 612 F.3d 1380, 1383–84 (Fed. Cir. 2010).

3.3.7 Prior Printed Publication

(Alleged infringer) contends that (challenged claim(s)) of (patent(s)) are invalid as anticipated because the invention defined in [that claim] [those claims] was described in a printed publication [more than one year before (named inventor(s)) filed the U.S. patent application on (U.S. filing date)] [before (named inventor(s)) invented the invention].

A patent claim is invalid if the invention defined by that claim was described in a printed publication [before it was invented by (named inventor(s))] [more than one year before the filing date of the U.S. application].

A printed publication must have been maintained in some tangible form whether in the United States or abroad, such as printed pages, typewritten pages, magnetic tape, microfilm, photographs, internet publication, photocopies, and the like, and must have been sufficiently accessible to persons interested in the subject matter of its contents.

Information is publicly accessible if it was distributed or otherwise made available to the extent that persons interested and ordinarily skilled in the subject matter exercising reasonable diligence can locate it. It is not necessary for the printed publication to have been available to every member of the public. An issued patent is a printed publication. A published patent application is a printed publication as of its publication date.

The disclosure of the claimed invention in the printed publication must be complete enough to enable one of ordinary skill in the art to use the invention without undue experimentation. In determining whether the disclosure is enabling, you should take into account what would have been within the knowledge of a person of ordinary skill in the art [one year before the application for the (abbreviated patent number) patent was filed] [at the time the invention of the (abbreviated patent number) patent was made], and you may consider evidence that sheds light on the knowledge such a person would have had.

Authorities

35 U.S.C. § 102(a), (b) (pre-AIA); 35 U.S.C. § 102(a)(1), (a)(2) (AIA); *In re Hall*, 781 F.2d 897, 898–99 (Fed. Cir. 1986); *In re Klopfenstein*, 380 F.3d 1345, 1352 (Fed. Cir. 2004); *In re Lister*, 583 F.3d 1307, 1311–12 (Fed. Cir. 2009); *Blue Calypso, LLC v. Groupon, Inc.*, 815 F.3d 1331, 1348–51 (Fed. Cir. 2016).

3.3.8 Inherency

Anticipation occurs if the invention claimed by the (asserted patent(s)) inherently and necessarily results from practice of what was disclosed in the prior art reference. There is no requirement that a person of ordinary skill in the art would have recognized the inherent disclosure at the time of invention, but only that the subject matter is in fact inherent in the prior art reference. A prior art reference may anticipate an undisclosed feature of the invention described in the prior art if that undisclosed feature is: (1) necessarily present in, or (2) the natural result of, the elements explicitly disclosed by the prior art. Inherency may not be established by probabilities or possibilities. There is no inherency when a certain thing may sometimes result from a given set of circumstances. Evidence outside of the prior art reference itself, including experimental testing, may be used to show that elements that are not expressly disclosed in the reference are inherent in it.

Authorities

Buildex, Inc. v. Kason Indus., Inc., 849 F.2d 1461, 1463 (Fed. Cir. 1988); *Cont'l Can Co. v. Monsanto Co.*, 948 F.2d 1264, 1267–69 (Fed. Cir. 1991); *Schering Corp. v. Geneva Pharm., Inc.*, 339 F.3d 1373, 1377–80 (Fed. Cir. 2003); *Toro Co. v. Deere & Co.*, 355 F.3d 1313, 1320–21 (Fed. Cir. 2004); *Net MoneyIN, Inc. v. Verisign, Inc.*, 545 F.3d 1359, 1369–70 (Fed. Cir. 2008).

3.4 Obviousness

Not all innovations are patentable. A patent claim is invalid if the claimed invention would have been obvious to a person of ordinary skill in the field at the time the application for (asserted patent(s)) was filed. This means that even if all of the requirements of the claim cannot be found in a single prior art reference that would anticipate the claim, a person of ordinary skill in the field of (identify field) who knew about all this prior art would have come up with the claimed invention. The following factors must be evaluated when determining whether (alleged infringer) has sufficiently established the claimed invention is obvious:

(1) The content and scope of the prior art presented by (alleged infringer);
(2) The differences between the claimed invention and the prior art;
(3) The level of ordinary skill in the art at the time of the invention; and
(4) Objective evidence, if any, which indicates the invention was obvious or nonobvious.

Each of the four factors must be evaluated separately for the claimed invention.

I will now explain each of the four factors in more detail.

Authorities

35 U.S.C. § 103; *KSR Int'l Co. v. Teleflex Inc.*, 550 U.S. 398, 407 (2007); *Graham v. John Deere Co.*, 383 U.S. 1, 17–18 (1966).

3.4.1 Factor 1: Content and Scope of Prior Art

The prior art you may consider is not limited to patents and published materials, but also includes the general knowledge that would have been available to a person having ordinary skill in the art or field of the invention. The scope and content of the prior art must be reasonably related to the claimed invention, such that a person having ordinary skill in the art would be aware of the art in the same field as the claimed invention or would look to a different field of invention that is relevant to the particular problem with which the claimed invention is concerned. You must determine what prior art is reasonably pertinent to the particular problems the inventor faced.

Authorities

35 U.S.C. § 103; *KSR Int'l Co. v. Teleflex Inc.*, 550 U.S. 398, 407 (2007); *In re Clay*, 966 F.2d 656, 658–59 (Fed. Cir. 1992).

3.4.2 Factor 2: Differences between the Claimed Invention and the Prior Art

When determining whether the claimed invention was obvious, each claim of the patent must be considered separately. However, you must view the differences between the claimed invention as a whole and the prior art as a person having ordinary skill in the art. You must take care to not use hindsight; when making the assessment, you may consider only what a person having ordinary skill in the art knew at the time of the invention.

Authorities

35 U.S.C. § 103; *KSR Int'l Co. v. Teleflex Inc.*, 550 U.S. 398, 407 (2007); *Graham v. John Deere Co.*, 383 U.S. 1, 17–18 (1966); *Arendi S.A.R.L. v. Apple Inc.*, 832 F.3d 1355, 1361–66 (Fed. Cir. 2016); *Par Pharm., Inc. v. TWI Pharm, Inc.*, 773 F.3d 1186, 1194–96 (Fed. Cir. 2014).

3.4.3 Factor 3: The Level of Ordinary Skill in the Art

The issue of obviousness is not whether the claimed invention would have been obvious to you as a layman or me as a judge or to a genius in the art, but rather whether it would have been obvious to a person having ordinary skill in the art or field of the invention at the time of the invention. The person having ordinary skill in the art is not the inventor, but rather a hypothetical person with ordinary creativity who knows all the prior art at the time of the invention. You have heard evidence as to what a person having ordinary skill in the art would be for the claimed invention. When determining the level of ordinary skill in the art or field of the invention, you should consider all the evidence introduced at trial, including but not limited to: (1) the level of education and experience of the inventor and other persons actively working in the field; (2) the types of problems encountered in the field at the time of the invention; (3) solutions to those problems in prior art; (4) the rapidity with which innovations were made in the field at the time of the invention; and (5) the sophistication of the technology at the time of the invention.

Authorities

35 U.S.C. § 103; *KSR Int'l Co. v. Teleflex Inc.*, 550 U.S. 398, 407 (2007); *Graham v. John Deere Co.*, 383 U.S. 1, 17–18 (1966); *Ruiz v. A.B. Chance Co.*, 234 F.3d 654, 665–67 (Fed. Cir. 2000).

3.4.4 Factor 4: Objective Evidence Indicating Non-Obviousness

Even when evidence sufficient to establish a fact or raise a presumption of obviousness has been presented, objective evidence of non-obviousness may nevertheless be sufficient to disprove a case of obviousness. You must evaluate facts related to the scope and content of the prior art, the differences between the invention and the prior art, the level of ordinary skill in the field of the invention, and objective considerations that indicate non-obviousness, providing there exists a link between the claimed invention and the objective evidence. No one factor is dispositive and you must consider the invention as a whole. You may consider any of the following factors that you find have been shown by the evidence:

(1) Whether the invention was commercially successful as a result of the merits of the claimed invention (rather than the result of design needs or market-pressure advertising or similar activities);
(2) Whether the invention satisfied a long-felt, but unresolved need;
(3) Whether others had tried and failed to make the invention;
(4) Whether others invented the invention at roughly the same time;
(5) Whether others copied the invention;

(6) Whether there were changes or related technologies or market needs at the same time as the invention;
(7) Whether the invention achieved unexpected results;
(8) Whether others in the field or industry praised the invention;
(9) Whether persons having ordinary skill in the art of the invention were skeptical and expressed surprise or disbelief regarding the invention;
(10) Whether others sought or obtained licensing rights to the patent from the patent holder; and
(11) Whether the inventor proceeded contrary to accepted wisdom in the field.

Finding that facts support any or all of these objective evidence factors may suggest the invention was not obvious.

3.4.4.1 Products Embodying the Patented Invention(s)

When you consider these factors, the (alleged infringer(s)) may show that the objective evidence is tied to a specific product. When the product embodies the claimed features of the asserted patent(s) and is coextensive with them you must presume, unless presented with credible evidence otherwise, that the patent claims are linked to a specific product and that product is the invention disclosed and claimed by the asserted patent(s).

On the other hand, when the product is not coextensive with the patented invention—for example, if the patented invention is only a component of a commercially successful machine or process—the patentee is not entitled to this presumption. However, even when the patent claims are not coextensive with a particular product, the (alleged infringer(s)) may still prove that the invention is not obvious based on these factors when evidence of secondary considerations is the direct result of the unique characteristics of the claimed invention.

3.4.4.2 Copying

The (alleged infringer(s)) may present evidence that the invention(s) [was] [were] copied. Copying requires duplication of features of the inventor's work based on access to that work. Copying requires proof that a specific product embodying the invention was copied. It is not enough to show that a similarity exists between the patent and a competitor's product. Evidence of copying may include, for example, internal documents, direct evidence such as photos of patented features or disassembly of products, or access and similarity to a patented product.

3.4.4.3 Industry Praise

The (alleged infringer(s)) may present evidence the invention(s) [was] [were] praised in the industry. Praise of the invention by those that are skilled in the field of the invention is a useful indicator of whether the invention would have been obvious to such persons at the time it was made. However, praise by those who are not skilled in the field is not sufficient to show that the invention is not obvious. Similarly, industry recognition of the achievement of the invention, such as awards, may suggest the invention is not obvious, provided that the praise is tied to the invention claimed by the patent.

3.4.4.4 Skepticism

The (alleged infringer(s)) may present evidence that there was skepticism in the industry surrounding the invention(s). If industry participants or those skilled in the field are skeptical about whether or how a problem could be solved or the workability of the claimed solution, it favors non-obviousness. Doubt or disbelief by those skilled in the field regarding the likely success of a combination or solution weighs against the notion that one would combine elements in references to achieve the claimed invention. Expressions of disbelief by experts constitute strong evidence that the invention is not obvious.

3.4.5 Other Considerations

There are additional considerations you can make when determining whether the invention(s) [was] [were] obvious. These considerations are whether the invention was obvious to try or if there was some motivation to combine the elements of the invention.

3.4.5.1 Consideration 1: Obvious to Try

Obviousness may be found when a known problem existed at the time of the invention for which there was an obvious solution that is covered by the claims of the patent. Similarly, an invention that merely applies a known technique that has been used to improve a similar device or method in a similar way may be proved obvious. Also obvious is an invention that would have been obvious to try; that is, the claimed innovation was merely one of a relatively small number of possible approaches to the problem with a reasonable expectation of success by a person having skill in the art.

Finding the invention to be obvious to try is insufficient if the art or technology is unpredictable. Conversely, the combination of familiar elements according to known methods is likely to be obvious when it does no more than yield predictable results. Design incentives and market forces can prompt variations to an invention in either the same field of endeavor or a different one. When determining obviousness, you must ask whether the invention is more than the predictable use of prior art elements according to their established functions.

3.4.5.2 Consideration 2: Motivation to Combine

When determining if a claimed invention is obvious, you may, but are not required to, find obviousness if you find that at the time of the claimed invention there was a reason that would have prompted a person having ordinary skill in the art or field of invention to combine the known elements of the invention in a way the claimed invention does. Accordingly, you may conduct a flexible analysis of whether there was some teaching, suggestion, or motivation for the inventor to arrive at the claimed invention at the time of the invention. However, proof of teaching, suggestion, or motivation for the invention is not required to prove obviousness.

Also, an invention with multiple elements is not proved obvious simply because each of those elements was known in the prior art. Teachings, suggestions, and motivations may be found explicitly or implicitly: (1) in the prior art references themselves; (2) in the knowledge of those persons having ordinary skill in the art that certain references, or disclosures in those references, that are of special interest or importance to the field; or (3) from the nature of the problem to be solved, which may lead inventors to look to references relating to the possible solutions to that problem. The references do not need to expressly teach that one disclosure should be combined with another; however, the ability to combine the disclosures must be clear and particular.

If prior art references teach away from combining certain known elements then discovery of a successful way of combining those elements is more likely not to be obvious. A reference may teach away when a person of ordinary skill, upon reading the reference, would be discouraged from following the path set out in the reference, or would be led in a direction divergent from the path that was taken by the inventor(s). But just because there are better alternatives to the patented invention taught in the prior art does not necessarily mean that following those alternatives would teach away from inferior alternatives.

Additionally, it is common sense that familiar items may have obvious uses beyond their primary purpose and a person having ordinary skill in the art will often be able to fit the teachings of multiple disclosures together like pieces of a puzzle. When combining disclosures to create an invention that is obvious to a person having ordinary skill in the art, some reasonable expectation of success should be present. A lack of a reasonable expectation of success or finding that prior art was teaching away from the combination of disclosures favors a determination that the invention was non-obvious.

Authorities

35 U.S.C. § 103; *KSR Int'l Co. v. Teleflex Inc.*, 550 U.S. 398, 407 (2007); *Graham v. John Deere Co.*, 383 U.S. 1, 17–18 (1966); Tr*ansocean Offshore Deepwater Drilling, Inc. v. Maersk Drilling USA, Inc.*, 699 F.3d 1340, 1349 (Fed. Cir. 2012); *Crocs, Inc. v. ITC*, 598 F.3d 1294, 1308 (Fed. Cir. 2010); *Comaper Corp. v. Antec, Inc.*, 596 F.3d 1343, 1352 (Fed. Cir. 2010); *Dippin' Dots, Inc. v. Mosey*, 476 F.3d 1337, 1343–44 (Fed. Cir. 2007); *Ruiz v. A.B. Chance Co.*, 234 F.3d 654, 665 (Fed. Cir. 2000); *Arkie Lures, Inc. v. Gene Larew Tackle, Inc.*, 119 F.3d 953, 955 (Fed. Cir. 1997); *In re Clay*, 966 F.2d 656, 658–59 (Fed. Cir. 1992); *Stratoflex, Inc. v. Aeroquip Corp.*, 713

F.2d 1530, 1538–40 (Fed. Cir. 1983); *Medtronic, Inc. v. Cardiac Pacemakers, Inc.*, 721 F.2d 1563, 1567–68 (Fed. Cir. 1983); *W.L. Gore & Assocs. v. Garlock, Inc.*, 721 F.2d 1540, 1555–56 (Fed. Cir. 1983).

3.5 Obviousness; Design Patents

A design patent claim is invalid if the claimed invention would have been obvious to a designer of ordinary skill in the field at the time the design was made. A person of ordinary skill is a designer of ordinary capability who designs articles of the type presented in the patent. Obviousness may be shown by considering more than one item of prior art. The ultimate conclusion of whether a claimed design is obvious should be based upon your determination of several factual decisions.

First, you must determine whether (alleged infringer) has identified a single prior art reference, or "primary reference," which creates basically the same overall visual impression as the claimed design as a whole.

If you identify a primary reference, you must then consider whether (alleged infringer) has identified one or more "secondary" prior art references that may be used to modify the primary reference to create a design that has the same overall visual appearance as the claimed design. "Secondary" references are other references that are so visually related to the primary reference that the appearance of certain ornamental features in the other references would suggest the application of those features to the primary reference. If you find that there are one or more such secondary references, you must determine if a designer of ordinary skill in these designs would have combined these references to create the same overall visual impression as the claimed design.

Finally, before deciding the issue of obviousness, you must consider other factors that might show that the designs were not obvious despite the prior art. You may only consider those factors that (alleged infringer) has established through the evidence admitted at trial.

(1) Were the products covered by the claimed design commercially successful due to the appearance of the claimed design?
(2) Did others copy the claimed design?

(3) Did the claimed design achieve an unexpectedly superior appearance of the closest prior art?
(4) Did others in the field praise the claimed design or express admiration for the claimed design?
(5) Did others seek or obtain licensing rights to the patent from the patent holder?

The presence of any one of the factors may be considered by you as an indication that the claimed invention would not have been obvious at the time that the claimed invention was made. Although you should consider any evidence of these factors, the relevance and importance of any of them to your decision on whether the claimed invention would have been obvious is up to you.

In deciding whether the claimed design was obvious, keep in mind that a design with several features is not obvious merely because each individual feature was present in prior art designs. You must always be careful not to determine obviousness using the benefit of hindsight. You should put yourself in the position of a person of ordinary skill in the field at the time the claimed design was made and should not consider what is known today.

Authorities

MRC Innovations, Inc. v. Hunter Mfg., LLP, 747 F.3d 1326, 1331 (Fed. Cir. 2014); *High Point Design LLC v. Buyers Direct, Inc.*, 730 F.3d 1301, 1311–15 (Fed. Cir. 2013); *Apple, Inc. v. Samsung Elec. Co.*, 678 F.3d 1314, 1329 (Fed. Cir. 2012); *Durling v. Spectrum Furniture Co.*, 101 F.3d 100, 103 (Fed. Cir. 1996); *Graham v. John Deere Co. of Kansas City*, 383 U.S. 1, 17, 86 S. Ct. 684, 694, 15 L. Ed. 2d 545 (1966); *In re Nalbandian*, 661 F.2d 1214, 1216 (C.C.P.A. 1981).

3.6 Written Description

(Alleged infringer) contends that (challenged claim(s)) of (patent(s)) are invalid as for failure to satisfy the written description requirement.

A patent must contain a written description of the [product] [process] claimed in the patent, though it is not required that the exact words found in the claim be used. When determining whether the specification discloses the invention, the claim must be viewed as a whole.

The written description requirement is satisfied if persons of ordinary skill in the field of the invention would recognize, from reading the patent specification, that the inventor possessed the subject matter claimed in the patent.

It is unnecessary to spell out every detail of the invention in the specification, and specific examples are not required. Only enough must be included in the specification to convince persons of ordinary skill in the art that the inventor possessed the full scope of the invention as of the date the application for patent was filed. The written description need not include information that is already known and available to the experienced public. In evaluating whether the specification has provided an adequate written description, you may take into account such factors as:

(1) the nature and scope of the patent claims;
(2) the complexity, predictability, and maturity of the technology at issue;
(3) the existing knowledge in the relevant field; and
(4) the scope and content of the prior art.

The issue of written description is decided on a claim-by-claim basis, not as to the entire patent or groups of claims. Thus, you are to decide this issue for each claim.

If you find that (alleged infringer) has proven that (challenged patent) does not contain a written description for the invention(s) of (challenged claims), then you must find that the claim(s) [is] [are] invalid.

Authorities

35 U.S.C. § 112; *Bard Peripheral Vascular, Inc. v. W.L. Gore & Assocs.*, 670 F.3d 1171, 1188–89 (Fed. Cir. 2012), *aff'd in part vacated in part remanded in part on reh'g*, 682 F.3d 1003, 1005 (Fed. Cir. 2012); *Streck,*

Inc. v. Research & Diagnostic Sys., 665 F.3d 1269, 1284–87 (Fed. Cir. 2012); *Atl. Research Mktg. Sys. v. Troy*, 659 F.3d 1345, 1353–55 (Fed. Cir. 2011); *Boston Sci. Corp. v. Johnson & Johnson*, 647 F.3d 1353, 1361–63 (Fed. Cir. 2011); *Crown Packaging Tech., Inc. v. Ball Metal Bev. Container Corp.*, 635 F.3d 1373, 1379–80 (Fed. Cir. 2011); *Centocor Ortho Biotech, Inc. v. Abbott Labs.*, 636 F.3d 1341, 1347–48 (Fed. Cir. 2011); *Ariad Pharms., Inc. v. Eli Lilly & Co.*, 598 F.3d 1336, 1351–52 (Fed. Cir. 2010) (en banc); *Research Corp. Techs. v. Microsoft Corp.*, 627 F.3d 859, 870 (Fed. Cir. 2010); *Laryngeal Mask Co. v. Ambu A/S*, 618 F.3d 1367, 1373–74 (Fed. Cir. 2010); *Revolution Eyewear, Inc. v. Aspex Eyewear, Inc.*, 563 F.3d 1358, 1366 (Fed. Cir. 2009); *PowerOasis, Inc. v. T-Mobile USA, Inc.*, 522 F.3d 1299, 1306 (Fed. Cir. 2008); *Faulkner v. Inglis*, 448 F.3d 1357, 1366 (Fed. Cir. 2006); *Kao Corp. v. Unilever United States, Inc.*, 441 F.3d 963, 968 (Fed. Cir. 2006); *Monsanto Co. v. Scruggs*, 459 F.3d 1328, 1336 (Fed. Cir. 2006); *Univ. of Rochester v. G.D. Searle & Co.*, 358 F.3d 916, 922–28 (Fed. Cir. 2004); *Enzo Biochem, Inc. v. Gen-Probe Inc.*, 323 F.3d 956, 964 (Fed. Cir. 2002); *Space Sys./Loral, Inc. v. Lockheed Martin Corp.*, 405 F.3d 985, 987 (Fed. Cir. 2005); *Enzo Biochem, Inc. v. Gen-Probe Inc.*, 323 F.3d 956, 970 (Fed. Cir. 2002); *Zoltek Corp. v. United States*, 815 F.3d 1302, 1308 (Fed. Cir. 2016).

3.7 Enablement

(Alleged infringer) contends that (challenged claim(s)) of (patent(s)) are invalid as for lack of enablement.

A patent must disclose sufficient information to enable or teach persons of ordinary skill in the field of the invention, at the time the [priority] patent application was filed, to make and use the full scope of the claimed invention without undue experimentation. This requirement is known as the *enablement requirement*. If a patent claim is not enabled, it is invalid.

In considering whether a patent complies with the enablement requirement, keep in mind that patents are written for persons of ordinary skill in the field of the invention. Thus, a patent need not expressly state information that persons of ordinary skill would already know.

The fact that some experimentation may be required for a person of ordinary skill to practice the claimed invention does not necessarily mean that a patent does not meet the enablement requirement. A patent does not need to guarantee that the invention works for a claim to be enabled. Similarly, a patentee is not required to provide actual working examples of the invention.

Factors that you may consider in determining whether persons of ordinary skill in the field of the invention would require undue experimentation to make and use the full scope of the claimed invention include:

(1) the quantity of experimentation necessary and whether that experimentation involves only known or commonly-used techniques;
(2) the amount of direction or guidance disclosed in the patent;
(3) the presence or absence of working examples in the patent;
(4) the nature of the invention;
(5) the state of the prior art;
(6) the relative skill of those in the art;
(7) the predictability of the art; and
(8) the breadth of the claims.

Authorities

35 U.S.C. § 112; *Streck, Inc. v. Research & Diagnostic Sys.*, 665 F.3d 1269, 1288–89 (Fed. Cir. 2012); *Transocean Offshore Deepwater Drilling, Inc. v. Maersk Contrs. USA, Inc.*, 617 F.3d 1296, 1305–07 (Fed. Cir. 2010); *ALZA Corp. v. Andrx Pharms., LLC*, 603 F.3d 935, 939–43 (Fed. Cir. 2010); *Martek Biosciences Corp. v. Nutrinova, Inc.*, 579 F.3d 1363, 1377–79 (Fed. Cir. 2009); *Sitrick v. Dreamworks, LLC*, 516 F.3d 993, 999–1002 (Fed. Cir. 2008); *Liebel-Flarsheim Co. v. Medrad, Inc.*, 481 F.3d 1371, 1380 (Fed. Cir. 2007); *AK Steel Corp. v. Sollac*, 344 F.3d 1234, 1244 (Fed. Cir. 2003); *Durel Corp. v. Osram Sylvania, Inc.*, 256 F.3d 1298, 1306 (Fed. Cir. 2001); *Union Pac. Res. Co. v. Chesapeake Energy Corp.*, 236 F.3d 684, 690–92 (Fed. Cir. 2001); *Ajinomoto Co. v. Archer-Daniels-Midland Co.*, 228 F.3d 1338, 1345–46 (Fed. Cir. 2000); *Nat'l Recovery Techs., Inc. v. Magnetic Separation Sys.*, 166 F.3d 1190, 1195–98 (Fed. Cir. 1999); *Enzo Biochem,*

Inc. v. Calgene, Inc., 188 F.3d 1362, 1371 (Fed. Cir. 1999); *In re Wands*, 858 F.2d 731, 737 (Fed. Cir. 1988); *Amgen, Inc. v. Chugai Pharm. Co.*, 927 F.2d 1200, 1213 (Fed. Cir. 1991).

3.8 Design Patents; Invalidity; Lack of Ornamentality

Design patents protect the ornamental appearance, including shape or configuration, of an article of manufacture. If (alleged infringer) proves that the overall appearance of (patent holder's) patented design is dictated by how the article claimed in the patent works, the patent is invalid because the design is not "ornamental."

When deciding this, you should keep in mind that design patents must be for articles of manufacture, which by definition have inherently functional characteristics. Simply because designs perform some function does not disqualify them from patent protection.

In determining whether a design is dictated by functionality, you may consider whether: (1) the protected design represents the best design; (2) alternative designs would adversely affect the utility of the specified article; (3) there are any related utility patents; (4) any advertising calls out particular features of the design as having specific utility; and (5) there are any elements in the design or an overall appearance clearly not dictated by function.

When there are several other designs that achieve the function of an article of manufacture, the design of the article is more likely to serve a primarily ornamental purpose. However, this may not be true if the other designs adversely affect the utility of the article.

Authorities

Egyptian Goddess, Inc. v. Swisa, Inc., 543 F.3d 665, 679 (Fed. Cir. 2008); *Sport Dimension, Inc. v. Coleman Co.*, 820 F.3d 1316, 1320 (Fed. Cir. 2016); *High Point Design LLC v. Buyers Direct, Inc.*, 730 F.3d 1301, 1315 (Fed. Cir. 2013); *L.A. Gear, Inc. v. Thom McAn Shoe Co.*, 988 F.2d 1117, 1123 (Fed. Cir. 1993); *PHG Techs., LLC v. St. John Co., Inc.*, 469 F.3d 1361, 1367 (Fed. Cir. 2006). *Rosco, Inc. v. Mirror Lite Co.*, 304 F.3d 1373, 1378 (Fed. Cir. 2002).

Chapter Four

DAMAGES

4.1 Background

4.1.1 Introduction to Damages

I have explained to you the law governing (patent holder's) allegation(s) of patent infringement and (alleged infringer's) defense(s) of noninfringement [and invalidity] [and unenforceability].

If you find that (patent holder) has proven that (alleged infringer) infringed any valid [and enforceable] claim of (asserted patent(s)), you must then determine what amount of damages (alleged infringer) must pay to (patent holder) to compensate (patent holder) for that infringement. If, on the other hand, you find that (patent holder) has not proven that (alleged infringer) infringed any valid [and enforceable] claim of (asserted patent(s)), then (patent holder) is not entitled to any damages, and you must not make any determination about damages.

You must keep in mind that, just because I will explain to you how to determine damages, I am not suggesting that either (patent holder) or (alleged infringer) has proven its allegations or defenses in this case. I am expressing no opinion one way or the other on the merits of those allegations or defenses. I am giving you this explanation about determining damages only to guide you if you find that (patent holder) has proven that (alleged infringer) infringed any valid [and enforceable] claim of (asserted patent(s)).

With that in mind, I will now explain to you how to determine damages.

Authorities

35 U.S.C. § 284; *Summit 6, LLC v. Samsung Elec. Co., Ltd.*, 802 F.3d 1283, 1296 (Fed. Cir. 2015); *Apple Inc. v. Motorola, Inc.*, 757 F.3d 1286, 1318 (Fed Cir. 2014), *overruled on other grounds by Williamson v. Citrix Online*, 792 F.3d 1339 (Fed. Cir. 2015) (en banc); *Dow Chem. Co. v. Mee Indus.*, 341 F.3d 1370, 1381 (Fed. Cir. 2003); *Integra Lifesciences I, LTD. v. Merck KGaA*, 331 F.3d 860, 870 (Fed. Cir. 2003); *Rite-Hite Corp. v. Kelley Co.*, 56 F.3d 1538, 1544–45 (Fed. Cir. 1995) (en banc).

4.1.2 Purpose of Damages

If you find that (patent holder) has proven that (alleged infringer) infringed any valid [and enforceable] claim of (asserted patent(s)), then (patent holder) is entitled to recover damages adequate to compensate (patent holder) for that infringement. In determining the amount of damages that would adequately compensate (patent holder) for that infringement, you must determine how much financial harm (patent holder) suffered as a result of that infringement.

You must keep in mind that the purpose of damages is to adequately compensate (patent holder) for any infringement of (asserted patent(s)) by (alleged infringer). To adequately compensate (patent holder), the amount of damages must put (patent holder) in approximately the same financial position that (patent holder) would have been in had (asserted patent(s)) not been infringed by (alleged infringer).

You must also keep in mind that damages are not intended to punish (alleged infringer) or to set an example.

Authorities

35 U.S.C. § 284; *Summit 6, LLC v. Samsung Elec. Co., Ltd.*, 802 F.3d 1283, 1296 (Fed. Cir. 2015); *Apple, Inc. v. Motorola, Inc.*, 757 F.3d 1286, 1318 (Fed Cir. 2014), *overruled on other grounds by Williamson v. Citrix Online*, 792 F.3d 1339 (Fed. Cir. 2015) (en banc); *Dow Chem. Co. v. Mee Indus.*, 341 F.3d 1370, 1381–82 (Fed. Cir. 2003); *Integra Lifesciences I, LTD. v. Merck KGaA*, 331 F.3d 860, 870 (Fed. Cir. 2003); *Grain Processing Corp. v. American Maize-Products Co.*, 185 F.3d 1341, 1349 (Fed. Cir. 1999); *Maxwell v. J. Baker, Inc.*, 86 F.3d 1098, 1108--09 (Fed. Cir. 1996); *Rite-Hite Corp. v. Kelley Co.*, 56 F.3d 1538, 1544–45 (Fed. Cir. 1995) (en banc).

4.1.3 Burden of Proof

(Patent holder) has the burden to prove the amount of damages that would put (patent holder) in approximately the same financial position that (patent holder) would have been in had (asserted patent(s)) not been infringed by (alleged infringer). (Patent holder) must prove the amount of damages by a preponderance of the evidence. That is, (patent holder) must show that it is more likely than not that (patent holder) suffered those damages.

Authorities

VirnetX, Inc. v. Cisco Sys., 767 F.3d 1308, 1326–27 (Fed. Cir. 2014); *Ericsson, Inc. v. D-Link Sys.*, 773 F.3d 1201, 1226 (Fed. Cir. 2014); *Uniloc USA, Inc. v. Microsoft Corp.*, 632 F.3d 1292, 1315 (Fed. Cir. 2011); *Lucent Techs., Inc. v. Gateway, Inc.*, 580 F.3d 1301, 1324 (Fed. Cir. 2009); *Vulcan Eng'g Co. v. FATA Aluminum, Inc.*, 278 F.3d 1366, 1376 (Fed. Cir. 2002).

4.1.4 Degree of Proof

(Patent holder) does not need to prove the amount of damages that (patent holder) suffered with mathematical precision. Rather, (patent holder) must prove the amount of damages that (patent holder) suffered with reasonable certainty. (Patent holder) is not entitled to recover any damages that are remote or speculative.

Authorities

Lucent Techs., Inc. v. Gateway, Inc., 580 F.3d 1301, 1340 (Fed. Cir. 2009); *Wechsler v. Macke Int'l Trade, Inc.*, 486 F.3d 1286, 1293–94 (Fed. Cir. 2007); *Micro Chem., Inc. v. Lextron, Inc.*, 318 F.3d 1119, 1125–26 (Fed. Cir. 2003); *Riles v. Shell Expl. & Prod. Co.*, 298 F.3d 1302, 1311 (Fed. Cir. 2002); *Minco, Inc. v. Combustion Eng'g, Inc.*, 95 F.3d 1109, 1118 (Fed. Cir. 1996); *Rite-Hite Corp. v. Kelley Co.*, 56 F.3d 1538, 1544–47 (Fed. Cir. 1995) (en banc); *Standard Havens Prods. v. Gencor Indus.*, 953 F.2d 1360, 1375 (Fed. Cir. 1991).

4.1.5 Role of Damages Experts

Experts called by (patent holder) and (alleged infringer) offered their opinions about the damages that (patent holder) allegedly suffered. The opinions of the damages experts, [identify damages experts by name], were based on the assumptions that (asserted patent(s)) is valid and that, without a license, (alleged infringer's) activities would have infringed (asserted patent(s)).

Therefore, because the damages experts' opinions were based on these assumptions, you must not infer anything about the validity of (asserted patent(s)) or infringement of (asserted patent(s)) based on the opinions of the damages experts.

Authorities

FED. R. EVID. 702; *VirnetX, Inc. v. Cisco Sys.*, 767 F.3d 1308, 1328 (Fed. Cir. 2014); *i4i Ltd. P'ship v. Microsoft Corp.*, 598 F.3d 831, 852–56 (Fed. Cir. 2010); *Lucent Techs., Inc. v. Gateway, Inc.*, 580 F.3d 1301, 1324–25 (Fed. Cir. 2009); *Georgia-Pacific Corp. v. United States Plywood Corp.*, 318 F. Supp. 1116, 1120 (S.D.N.Y. 1970), *judgment modified by* 446 F.2d 295 (2d Cir. 1971).

4.2 Date Damages Begin

[Three alternative instructions are provided based on the circumstances of the case. The following instruction should be given in the event the parties agree on the date for commencement of damages.]

If you find that (patent holder) has proven that (alleged infringer) infringed any valid [and enforceable] claim of (asserted patent(s)), you should assess damages beginning on (insert date). (Patent owner) and (alleged infringer) have agreed upon this date.

[The following alternative instruction should be given in the event the parties agree that the marking requirement was satisfied or does not apply.]

If you find that (patent holder) has proven that (alleged infringer) infringed any valid [and enforceable] claim of (asserted patent(s)), the first step in determining the amount of damages that (patent holder) is entitled to is to determine the date on which damages started. The damages period begins on the date the patent issued, the date the alleged infringement began, or six years prior to the filing of this lawsuit, whichever is later.

[The following instruction should be given in the event the parties disagree that the marking requirement applies and/or was satisfied.]

If you find that (patent holder)] has proven that (alleged infringer) infringed any valid [and enforceable] claim of (asserted patent(s)), the first step in determining the amount of damages that (patent holder) is entitled to is to determine the date on which damages started.

If (patent holder) [or its licensees] made, offered for sale, or sold products that practice (asserted patent(s)) in the United States, and (patent holder) is asserting product, apparatus, or system claims, (patent holder) is entitled to recover damages only for infringement that occurred after (patent holder) gave notice of its patent rights. One way (patent holder) could have given notice of its patent rights is by giving actual notice to (alleged infringer). (Patent holder) could have given actual notice to (alleged infringer) by notifying (alleged infringer) that (alleged infringer) was allegedly infringing (asserted patent(s)) and by identifying (alleged infringer's) products that allegedly infringed (asserted patent(s)). This way of giving actual notice to (alleged infringer) is effective on the date (patent holder) gave such notice to (alleged infringer). The other type of notice is marking, which I will discuss next.

Note

In determining when damages begin for method claims, there is no notice requirement. 35 U.S.C. § 287(2)(F); *Am. Med. Sys. v. Med. Eng'g Corp.*, 6 F.3d 1523, 1538 (Fed. Cir. 1993) ("The law is clear that the notice provisions of section 287 do not apply where the patent is directed to a process or method."). Thus, the calculation of damages for infringement of method claims should begin as of the date the patent issued or the date on which the alleged infringement began, whichever is later. *Crystal Semiconductor Corp. v. Tritech Microelectronics Int'l, Inc.*, 246 F.3d 1336, 1353 (Fed. Cir. 2001). When a patent contains both apparatus and method claims, the patent owner and any licensee are required to mark embodying products with the patent. *Am. Med. Sys.*, 6 F.3d at 1538. However, where the patentee only asserts the method claims of such a patent, the marking requirement does not apply. *Crown Packaging Tech., Inc. v. Rexam Bev. Can Co.*, 559 F.3d 1308, 1317 (Fed. Cir. 2009).

Authorities

35 U.S.C. §§ 286, 287; *Iron Oak Techs., LLC v. Microsoft Corp.*, 817 Fed. App'x 955 (Fed. Cir. 2020) (patentee did not provide notice to defendant when notice letters were sent to manufacturers that included defendant's product in their final products and not to defendant); *SCA Hygiene Prods. Aktiebolag v. First Quality Baby Prods.*, LLC, 137 S. Ct. 954, 976 (2017) ("Laches cannot be interposed as a defense against damages where the infringement occurred within the period prescribed by [35 U.S.C.] § 286."); *Arctic Cat, Inc. v. Bombardier Recreational Prod.*, 876 F.3d 1350, 1365–66 (Fed. Cir. 2017); *SRI Int'l, Inc. v. Advanced Tech. Labs., Inc.*, 127 F.3d 1462, 1470 (Fed. Cir. 1997).

4.3 Notice Requirement for Product Claims

[The following instruction should be given only if the patent holder or its licensee(s) made, used, or sold a product that embodies or practices an invention covered by the asserted patent. There is no notice requirement for patents that claim only processes or methods. *See Crown Packaging Tech., Inc. v. Rexam Bev. Can Co.*, 559 F.3d 1308, 1316 (Fed. Cir. 2009); *Crystal Semiconductor Corp. v. Tritech Microelectronics Int'l, Inc.*, 246 F. 3d 1336, 1353 (Fed. Cir. 2001). If the patent holder asserts both product and

process or method claims, and there is an embodying product to mark, the patent holder is required to give notice of its patent rights. *Crown Packaging*, 559 F.3d at 1316–17.]

The other way that (patent holder) could have given notice of its patent rights is by giving notice to the general public by marking products it [made] [used] [sold] [imported] with the word "Patent" or the abbreviation "Pat." and the number of (the asserted patent(s)) or a free internet address which associates (patent holder's) products with the patent number of (asserted patent(s)). The free internet address may be listed on the product packaging or label if not feasible to list it on the actual product. This way of giving notice to the general public is effective on the date that (patent holder) started to mark substantially all of the products that embody, or practice, the patented invention.

The burden is on (patent holder) to show that it has marked substantially all of its products that practice the patented invention. In addition, once marking has begun, it must be substantially continuous. If (alleged infringer) identifies any of (patent holder's) products that it alleges embody the patented invention but were not marked, (patent holder) bears the burden of proving that those products did not embody the patented invention and therefore did not need to be marked. If you find that (patent holder) has not met its burden of showing that its products did not need to be marked, then damages do not accrue until (patent holder) provided actual notice to (alleged infringer) of the asserted patents.

If (patent holder) has licensed the asserted patent(s) and the licensee makes or sells a product that practices the patent(s), then the requirement to mark extends to the licensee. To satisfy the marking requirement where a licensee and not the patent holder makes or sells a product that practices the patent(s), (patent holder) must have made reasonable efforts to ensure its licensee complied with the marking requirement.

To summarize, (patent holder) is entitled to recover damages only for infringement that occurred after (patent holder) gave notice of its patent rights either by giving notice to the general public through marking (patent holder/licensee's) products or by giving actual notice to (alleged infringer), as I have just explained.

If you find that (patent holder) did not give notice to the general public or actual notice to (alleged infringer), then (patent holder) is entitled to recover damages only for infringement that occurred after it filed this lawsuit on (date).

Note

Damages for infringement of process or method claims start when the patent has issued and infringement has occurred. *Crystal Semiconductor*, 246 F.3d at 1353. If an alleged infringer identifies potential unmarked patented articles subject to the notice requirements of Section 287, the alleged infringer does not need to prove that those products practice the claimed invention; instead, the burden shifts to the patent holder to prove that the identified products do not practice the claimed invention. *Arctic Cat, Inc. v. Bombardier Rec. Prod.*, 950 F.3d 860, 863 (Fed. Cir. 2020). If the patent holder or its licensee failed to mark patent-practicing products, Section 287 continues to limit damages even after the patent holder or its licensee ceases the manufacture or sale of any unmarked products, until notice is provided. *Id.* at 862.

Authorities

35 U.S.C. § 287; *Arctic Cat, Inc. v. Bombardier Rec. Prods.*, 950 F.3d 860, 862 (Fed. Cir. 2020); *Packet Intelligence LLC v. NetScout Sys.*, 965 F.3d 1299, 1312–14 (Fed. Cir. 2020); *Arctic Cat, Inc. v. Bombardier Rec. Prods.*, 876 F.3d 1350, 1366 (Fed. Cir. 2017); *ActiveVideo Networks, Inc. v. Verizon Commc'ns, Inc.*, 694 F.3d 1312, 1333–34 (Fed. Cir. 2012); *Crown Packaging Tech., Inc. v. Rexam Bev. Can Co.*, 559 F.3d 1308, 1316–17 (Fed. Cir. 2009); *Crystal Semiconductor Corp. v. Tritech Microelectronics Int'l, Inc.*, 246 F.3d 1336, 1353 (Fed. Cir. 2001); *Nike Inc. v. Wal-Mart Stores, Inc.*, 138 F.3d 1437, 1443–44 (Fed. Cir. 1998); *Maxwell v. J. Baker, Inc.*, 86 F.3d 1098, 1111–-12 (Fed. Cir. 1996); *Am. Med. Sys. v. Med. Eng'g Corp.*, 6 F.3d 1523, 1537–38 (Fed. Cir. 1993).

4.4 Two Types of Damages: Lost Profits and a Reasonable Royalty

There are two types of damages for patent infringement. The first type of damages is called lost profits. In general, lost profits damages compensate a patent holder for the profits that the patent holder would have made if the patent holder's patent had not been infringed. I will explain lost profits to you in more detail.

The second type of damages is called a reasonable royalty. In general, a reasonable royalty is the amount of money that a reasonable person would agree to pay, and a reasonable patent holder would agree to accept for the right to [make] [use] [sell] [import] the invention covered by the patent holder's patent. I will also explain a reasonable royalty to you in more detail after I explain lost profits to you.

Authorities

35 U.S.C. § 284; *Warsaw Orthopedic, Inc. v. NuVasive, Inc.*, 778 F.3d 1365, 1373–79 (Fed. Cir. 2015), *vacated and remanded by Medtronic Sofamor Danek USA, Inc. v. NuVasive, Inc.*, 577 U.S. 1099 (2016) (Mem.), *reaff'd in relevant part, Warsaw Orthopedic, Inc. v. NuVasive, Inc.*, 824 F.3d 1344, 1351 (Fed. Cir. 2016); *Siemens Med. Sols. USA, Inc. v. Saint-Gobain Ceramics & Plastics, Inc.*, 637 F.3d 1269, 1288–89 (Fed. Cir. 2011); *Crystal Semiconductor Corp. v. Tritech Microelectronics Int'l, Inc.*, 246 F.3d 1336, 1354 (Fed. Cir. 2001); *Grain Processing Corp. v. Am. Maize-Products Co.*, 185 F.3d 1341, 1349 (Fed. Cir. 1999); *Tec Air, Inc. v. Denso Mfg. Mich., Inc.*, 192 F.3d 1353, 1362 (Fed. Cir. 1999); *Fonar Corp. v. GE*, 107 F.3d 1543, 1553 (Fed. Cir. 1997); *Oiness v. Walgreen Co.*, 88 F.3d 1025, 1029 (Fed. Cir. 1996); *Zygo Corp. v. Wyko Corp.*, 79 F.3d 1563, 1571 (Fed. Cir. 1996); *Rite-Hite Corp. v. Kelley Co.*, 56 F.3d 1538, 1545 (Fed. Cir. 1995) (en banc); *BIC Leisure Prods. v. Windsurfing Int'l*, 1 F.3d 1214, 1218 (Fed. Cir. 1993); *Smithkline Diagnostics, Inc. v. Helena Labs. Corp.*, 926 F.2d 1161, 1164 (Fed. Cir. 1991).

4.5 Lost Profits

[These instructions should be given only if the patent holder is seeking lost profits damages.]

4.5.1 Lost Profits; Generally

In this case, (patent holder) is seeking to recover lost profits damages. In general, lost profits damages are the additional profits that a patent holder would have made if an alleged infringer had not made infringing sales.

4.5.2 Lost Profits; "But for" Causation

(Patent holder) claims that, if (alleged infringer) had not infringed (asserted patent(s)), [(patent holder) would have made all [or a portion] of the alleged infringing sales made by (alleged infringer)], [(patent holder) would have sold additional products not containing the invention covered by (asserted patent(s))], [and] [or] [(patent holder) would have sold products containing the invention covered by (asserted patent(s)) at a higher price].

When basing alleged lost profits on lost sales, (patent holder) has the initial burden of proving that there is a reasonable probability it would have made additional sales "but for" (alleged infringer's) infringement of (asserted patent(s)). That is, (patent holder) must prove that, if (alleged infringer) had not sold (accused product), it is reasonably likely that (patent holder) would have made all or a portion of those alleged infringing sales.

If (patent holder) proves that, "but for" (alleged infringer's) infringement of (asserted patent(s)), (patent holder) would have made all or a portion of these sales, the burden then shifts to (alleged infringer) to prove that (patent holder) would not have made some or all of the alleged infringing sales.

Authorities

Aro Mfg. Co. v. Convertible Top Replacement Co., 377 U.S. 476 (1964); *Mentor Graphics Corp. v. EVE-USA, Inc.*, 851 F.3d 1275, 1284–85 (Fed. Cir. 2017); *Siemens Med. Sols. USA, Inc. v. Saint-Gobain Ceramics & Plastics, Inc.*, 637 F.3d 1269, 1287 (Fed Cir. 2011); *Am. Seating Co. v. USSC*

Grp., Inc., 514 F.3d 1262, 1269 (Fed. Cir. 2008); *Grain Processing Corp. v. American Maize-Products Co.*, 185 F.3d 1341, 1349 (Fed. Cir. 1999); *Rite-Hite Corp. v. Kelley Co.*, 56 F.3d 1538, 1545 (Fed. Cir. 1995) (en banc).

4.5.3 Lost Profits; Non-Exclusive Factors

There is no particular or required method to prove (alleged infringer) caused (patent holder's) lost profits. However, one way (patent holder) can prove that it would have made [additional] sales absent infringement is by proving four things. I will now tell you what those four things are, and then go back and explain each one to you in more detail.

First, there was demand for the product that contains the invention covered by (asserted patent(s)).

Second, there was no acceptable, non-infringing substitute for the patented invention.

Third, (patent holder) had the ability to make the allegedly infringing sales made by (alleged infringer). In other words, (patent holder) was capable of satisfying the demand for these additional sales.

Fourth, the amount of profits (patent holder) would have made, had it made the sales rather than (alleged infringer).

I will now explain what each of these four things means.

4.5.3.1 Lost Profits; Demand

The first thing you should consider is whether there was demand for the product that contains the invention covered by (asserted patent(s)). I will refer to this as the "patented product," but it also includes patented methods or products produced by patented methods. In making this determination, you should consider whether there was demand for the product as a whole, not just demand for the patented parts or features.

(Patent holder) can prove demand for the patented product by showing significant sales of (patent holder's) patented product or by showing significant infringing sales by (alleged infringer). To use infringing sales as proof of demand, the patented product and (accused product) must be similar enough to compete against each other.

Authorities

Mentor Graphics Corp. v. EVE-USA, Inc., 851 F.3d 1275, 1285 (Fed. Cir. 2017); *Depuy Spine, Inc. v. Medtronic Sofamor Danek, Inc.*, 567 F.3d 1314, 1330 (Fed. Cir. 2009); *Rite-Hite Corp. v. Kelley Co.*, 56 F.3d 1538, 1546, 1548–49 (Fed. Cir. 1995); *BIC Leisure Prods., Inc. v. Windsurfing Int'l*, 1 F.3d 1214, 1218–19 (Fed. Cir. 1993); *Smithkline Diagnostics, Inc. v. Helena Labs. Corp.*, 926 F.2d 1161, 1165 n.3 (Fed. Cir. 1991); *Gyromat Corp. v. Champion Spark Plug Co.*, 735 F.2d 549, 552 (Fed. Cir. 1984).

4.5.3.2 Lost Profits; Non-Infringing Substitute; Acceptability

The second thing you should consider is whether there was an acceptable, non-infringing substitute for (patent holder's) patented product. To be an acceptable, non-infringing substitute, a product must have the advantages of the invention covered by (asserted patent(s)) that were important to those who purchased (accused product). If purchasers of (accused product) were motivated to buy (accused product) because of patented features available only in (accused product) and (patent holder's) patented product, then some other product is not an acceptable substitute. This is so even if the other product competed with (accused product) and (patent holder's) patented product. On the other hand, if non-infringing competitors would likely have captured the infringing sales made by (alleged infringer), then (patent holder) is not entitled to lost profits damages based on those sales.

Authorities

Presidio Components, Inc. v. Am. Tech. Ceramics Corp., 702 F.3d 1351, 1361 (Fed. Cir. 2012); *Am. Seating Co. v. USSC Grp., Inc.*, 514 F.3d 1262, 1270 (Fed. Cir. 2008) ("[B]uyers must view the substitute as equivalent to the patented device."); *Tate Access Floors, Inc. v. Maxcess Techs., Inc.*, 222 F.3d 958, 971 (Fed. Cir. 2000); *Grain Processing Corp. v. Am. Maize-Prod. Co.*, 185 F.3d 1341, 1349 (Fed. Cir. 1999); *Gargoyles, Inc. v. United States*, 113 F.3d 1572, 1577–78 (Fed. Cir. 1997); *Stryker Corp. v. Intermedics Orthopedics, Inc.*, 96 F.3d 1409, 1417–18 (Fed. Cir. 1996); *Rite-Hite*

Corp. v. Kelley Co., 56 F.3d 1538, 1548 (Fed. Cir. 1995) (en banc); *Uniroyal, Inc. v. Rudkin-Wiley Corp.*, 939 F.2d 1540, 1545–46 (Fed. Cir. 1991); *Std. Havens Prod. v. Gencor Indus.*, 953 F.2d 1360, 1373 (Fed. Cir. 1991); *Smithkline Diagnostics, Inc. v. Helena Labs. Corp.*, 926 F.2d 1161, 1166 (Fed. Cir. 1991); *Slimfold Mfg. Co. v. Kinkead Indus.*, 932 F.2d 1453 (Fed. Cir. 1991); *Kaufman Co. v. Lantech, Inc.*, 926 F.2d 1136, 1142 (Fed. Cir. 1991); *State Indus., Inc. v. Mor-Flo Indus., Inc.*, 883 F.2d 1573, 1576–77 (Fed. Cir. 1989).

4.5.3.3 Lost Profits; Non-Infringing Substitute; Availability

[The following instruction should be given only if the alleged infringer claims that there were non-infringing substitutes that were available, but not sold in the relevant market.]

When considering whether acceptable, non-infringing substitutes for (accused product) and the patented product were available, you should consider whether any alleged substitute was actually sold in the relevant market during that time.

If the alleged substitute was not sold in the market, you may infer that it was not available as a substitute. (Alleged infringer) may overcome this inference by showing that the alleged substitute was in fact available during this period. Mere speculation or conclusory assertions will not suffice to overcome the inference, though.

When an alleged substitute was not on the market at the time of the damages period, but could have been under different circumstances, you may consider factors such as the ease with which a substitute was eventually made available, the state of the technology, and the availability of input products and equipment to make the substitute. If the material, experience, and know-how for the alleged substitute were readily available at the time of infringement, that may suggest the substitute was available. If, however, the material was of such high cost as to render the alternative unfeasible, or (the alleged infringer) had to dedicate significant resources to design or invent around the patented technology to develop an alleged substitute, that may suggest the substitute was unavailable.

That said, just because the alleged substitute was not widely advertised, or was available only to a limited set of customers, does not necessarily render the substitute unavailable.

Authorities

Presidio Components, Inc. v. Am. Tech. Ceramics Corp., 875 F.3d 1369, 1381 (Fed. Cir. 2017) (finding limited-availability alternative may have been more widely available in a world without the infringing product); *Synqor, Inc. v. Artesyn Techs., Inc.*, 709 F.3d 1365, 1382 (Fed. Cir. 2013); *Siemens Med. Sols. USA, Inc. v. Saint-Gobain Ceramics & Plastics, Inc.*, 637 F.3d 1269, 1288 (Fed. Cir. 2011) ("A substitute need not be on sale at the time of infringement, but if the substitute cannot be commercialized 'readily,' then it is not available for purposes of a lost profits determination."); *Micro Chem., Inc. v. Lextron, Inc.*, 318 F.3d 1119 (Fed Cir. 2003); *Grain Processing Corp. v. Am. Maize-Products Co.*, 185 F.3d 1341, 1353 (Fed. Cir. 1999).

4.5.3.4 Lost Profits; Capability

The third thing you should consider is whether (patent holder) had the manufacturing and marketing capabilities to make the sales that (patent holder) claims that it lost due to (alleged infringer's) infringement of (asserted patent(s)). A patent holder is entitled to lost profits only for sales that it could have actually made. Thus, (patent holder) must prove that it had the manufacturing and marketing capabilities to make the sales that (patent holder) allegedly lost. This means (patent holder) must prove that it could have made and sold, or could have had someone else make or sell, the additional products.

Authorities

Wechsler v. Macke Int'l Trade, Inc., 486 F.3d 1286, 1293 (Fed. Cir. 2007); *Gargoyles, Inc. v. United States*, 113 F.3d 1572, 1577–78 (Fed. Cir. 1997); *Fonar Corp. v. GE*, 107 F.3d 1543, 1553 (Fed. Cir. 1997); *Kearns v. Chrysler Corp.*, 32 F.3d 1541, 1551 (Fed. Cir. 1994); *Datascope Corp. v. SMEC, Inc.*, 879 F.2d 820, 825 (Fed. Cir. 1989); *Gyromat Corp. v. Champion Spark Plug Co.*, 735 F.2d 549, 554 (Fed. Cir. 1984).

4.5.3.5 Lost Profits; Calculation of Amount

The fourth thing you should consider is the amount of profits (patent holder) allegedly lost as a result of the lost sales that it has proven.

4.5.4 Lost Profits; Market Share

I will now explain how to calculate the amount of lost sales when there is a non-infringing substitute. If you find that there were acceptable, available non-infringing substitutes in the relevant market, (patent holder) may still be entitled to lost profits damages on a portion of (alleged infringer's) infringing sales if (patent holder) proves that the patented product competed in the same market as (accused product), and that (patent holder) would have made a portion of (alleged infringer's) infringing sales.

One way (patent holder) may prove the portion of sales that it would have made if (alleged infringer) had not infringed (asserted patent(s)) is to show its share of the relevant market without the infringing sales. If (patent holder) proves its market share, you may find that (patent holder's) lost sales are the percentage of (alleged infringer's) infringing sales equal to (patent holder's) market share.

In determining (patent holder's) market share, you should decide which products are in the same relevant market. Products are in the same market if they are sufficiently similar to compete against each other.

Authorities

Ericsson, Inc. v. Harris Corp., 352 F.3d 1369, 1377–78 (Fed. Cir. 2003); *Micro Chem., Inc. v. Lextron, Inc.*, 318 F.3d 1119, 1124 (Fed. Cir. 2003); *Crystal Semiconductor Corp. v. Tritech Microelectronics Int'l, Inc.*, 246 F.3d 1336, 1354–56 (Fed. Cir. 2001); *BIC Leisure Prods., Inc. v. Windsurfing Int'l*, 1 F.3d 1214, 1218–19 (Fed. Cir. 1993); *State Indus., Inc. v. Mor-Flo Indus., Inc.*, 883 F.2d 1573, 1577–78 (Fed. Cir. 1989). Price disparity does not necessarily preclude an award of lost profits, so long as there is a reasonable factual basis accounting for the disparity. *See Akamai Techs., Inc. v. Limelight Networks, Inc.*, 805 F.3d 1368, 1380 (Fed. Cir. 2015) (rejecting alleged infringers argument that price disparity precluded lost profits award, as the expert reasonably accounted for the disparity and market elasticity).

4.5.5 Lost Profits; Two-Supplier Market

Another way for (patent holder) to prove that it would have made additional sales of its patented product "but for" (alleged infringer's) infringement, is by showing two things.

First, that (patent holder) and (alleged infringer) are the only suppliers for the product in the relevant market.

Second, that (patent holder) was capable of making all of the allegedly infringing sales made by (alleged infringer).

If (patent holder) proves these two things, then (patent holder) is entitled to recover its lost profits on all of the infringing sales made by (alleged infringer).

In determining whether (patent holder) and (alleged infringer) are the only suppliers for the product in the relevant market, you should decide if the products are in the same relevant market. Products are in the same market if they are sufficiently similar to compete against each other.

Note

Where there are only two suppliers in the relevant product market, it may be inferred that the patent holder would have made the alleged infringer's infringing sales, unless the alleged infringer can overcome the inference.

Price disparity in a two-supplier market does not necessarily preclude an award of lost profits, so long as there is a reasonable factual basis accounting for the disparity. *See Akamai Techs., Inc. v. Limelight Networks, Inc.*, 805 F.3d 1368, 1380 (Fed. Cir. 2015) (rejecting alleged infringers argument that price disparity precluded lost profits award, as the expert reasonably accounted for the disparity and market elasticity).

Authorities

TEK Glob., S.R.L. v. Sealant Sys. Int'l, 920 F.3d 777, 790 (Fed. Cir. 2019); *WesternGeco L.L.C. v. ION Geophysical Corp.*, 913 F.3d 1067, 1072 (Fed. Cir. 2019); *Siemens Med. Sols. USA, Inc. v. Saint-Gobain Ceramics & Plastics, Inc.*, 637 F.3d 1269, 1288 (Fed. Cir. 2011); *Micro Chem., Inc.*

v. Lextron, Inc., 318 F.3d 1119, 1124–25 (Fed. Cir. 2003); *Kaufman Co. v. Lantech, Inc.*, 926 F.2d 1136, 1141 (Fed. Cir. 1991); *Lam, Inc. v. Johns-Manville Corp.*, 718 F.2d 1056, 1065 (Fed. Cir. 1983).

4.5.6 Lost Profits; Convoyed Sales

[The following instruction should be given only if the patent holder is seeking lost profits based on convoyed sales.]

In this case, (patent holder) is [also] seeking lost profits based on sales of products that do not contain the invention covered by (asserted patent(s)). (Patent holder) claims that it would have sold these products together with the patented product. For simplicity, I will call these additional products "other products."

To recover lost profits based on sales of these other products, (patent holder) must prove two things.

First, (patent holder) must prove that (patent holder) would have sold the other products but for the infringement by (alleged infringer).

Second, (patent holder) must prove that the other products and the patented product or component function together to produce a desired result. The products or components must be like components of a single assembly, or parts of a complete machine, or they must constitute a single functional unit.

Recovery for lost profits on sales of other products should not include products that do not function with the product containing the patented invention and that are sold with the product containing the patented invention merely for the convenience of (patent holder).

Authorities

Depuy Spine, Inc. v. Medtronic Sofamor Danek, Inc., 567 F.3d 1314, 1333 (Fed. Cir. 2009); *Am. Seating Co. v. USSC Grp., Inc.*, 514 F.3d 1262, 1268 (Fed. Cir. 2008); *Rite-Hite Corp. v. Kelley Co.*, 56 F.3d 1538, 1550 (Fed. Cir. 1995) (en banc) (denying recovery for lost profits on collateral sales where nonpatented product lacked a functional relationship to the patented product); *see also State Indus., Inc. v. Mar-Flo Indus., Inc.*, 883 F.2d 1573, 1580 (Fed. Cir. 1989); *Panduit Corp. v. Stahlin Bros. Fibre Works*, 575 F.2d 1152, 1157–58 (6th Cir. 1978).

4.5.7 Lost Profits; Calculation of Amount

(Patent holder) must also prove the amount of profits that it allegedly lost as a result of the lost sales that it has proven. Profits are determined by deducting certain costs from the revenue that (patent holder) would have received from a sale. Therefore, to determine (patent holder's) lost profits, you should, for example, deduct (patent holder's) cost of goods from the revenue that (patent holder) would have received from a sale. Costs might also include additional costs for making the products and additional sales costs, such as packaging, shipping, or other costs. Any costs that do not change when more products are made, such as fixed taxes, insurance, rent, and administrative overhead, should not be subtracted from the lost sales amount.

Note

Lost profits may generally only be recovered for those sales that would have occurred within the United States. A patent holder is not entitled to any lost profits for any foreign sales that it may have made, even if those foreign sales were foreseeable at the time of infringement. *Power Integrations, Inc. v. Fairchild Semiconductor Int'l, Inc.*, 711 F.3d 1348, 1370–71 (Fed. Cir. 2013). This general rule is subject to one exception: if the patent holder has proven that the alleged infringer's shipment in or from the United States of components especially made or adapted for use in the patented invention, with the intent that such components were to be combined outside the United States in a manner that would infringe the asserted patents if such combination occurred within the United States, the patent holder may also be entitled to lost profits for any foreign sales caused by such infringement. *WesternGeco LLC v. ION Geophysical Corp.*, 138 S. Ct. 2129, 2138 (2018) (patentee can recover lost profits from foreign sales that infringe under 35 U.S.C. § 271(f)(2)). While the holding of *WesternGeco* was limited to § 271(f)(2), at least one district court has held that *WesternGeco* implicitly overruled *Power Integrations*, suggesting that recovery may be permitted for other types of infringement under § 271. *See Power Integrations, Inc. v. Fairchild Semiconductor Int'l, Inc.*, No. CV 04-1371-LPS, 2018 WL 4804685, at *1 (D. Del. Oct. 4, 2018); *but see MLC Intellectual Prop., LLC v. Micron Tech., Inc.*, No. 14-CV-03657-SI, 2019 WL 2437073, at *3 (N.D. Cal. June 11, 2019).

Authorities

Versata Software, Inc. v. SAP Am., Inc., 717 F.3d 1255, 1266–67 (Fed. Cir. 2013) (affirming jury award of lost profits in which the value of each lost sale took into account additional costs associated with making the sales); *Sensonics, Inc. v. Aerosonic Corp.*, 81 F.3d 1566, 1572 (Fed. Cir. 1996); *Oiness v. Walgreen Co.*, 88 F.3d 1025, 1030 (Fed. Cir. 1996); *Beatrice Foods Co. v. New Eng. Printing & Litho. Co.*, 923 F.2d 1576, 1579 (Fed. Cir. 1991); *Kalman v. Berlyn Corp.*, 914 F.2d 1473, 1482–83 (Fed. Cir. 1990); *State Indus., Inc. v. Mor-Flo Indus., Inc.*, 883 F.2d 1573, 1579–80 (Fed. Cir. 1989); *Ryco, Inc. v. Ag-Bag Corp.*, 857 F.2d 1418, 1428 (Fed. Cir. 1988); *Del Mar Avionics, Inc. v. Quinton Instrument Co.*, 836 F.2d 1320, 1327 (Fed. Cir. 1987); *King Instrument Corp. v. Otari Corp.*, 767 F.2d 853, 863–64 (Fed. Cir. 1985); *Gyromat Corp. v. Champion Spark Plug Co.*, 735 F.2d 549, 554–55 (Fed. Cir. 1984); *Paper Converting Mach. Co. v. Magna-Graphics Corp.*, 745 F.2d 11, 22 (Fed. Cir. 1984); *Bio-Rad Labs., Inc. v. Nicolet Instrument Corp.*, 739 F.2d 604 (Fed. Cir. 1984); *Lam, Inc. v. Johns-Manville Corp.*, 718 F.2d 1056, 1065 (Fed. Cir. 1983)

4.5.8 Lost Profits; Price Erosion

[The following instruction should be given only if the patent holder claims that it should be compensated for price erosion.]

(Patent holder) may recover additional damages if it proves that, had (alleged infringer) not infringed (asserted patent(s)), (patent holder) would have been able to charge higher prices for the product containing the invention covered by the patent. If you find that (patent holder) has proven this, you may award as additional damages to (patent holder) the difference between:

(1) The amount of profits (patent holder) would have made by selling the product containing the invention at the higher price, and
(2) The amount of profits (patent holder) actually made by selling the product containing the invention at the lower price (patent holder) actually charged for its product.

These damages are called "price-erosion damages."

If you find that (patent holder) suffered price-erosion damages, you may also use the higher price in determining (patent holder's) lost profits from sales that were lost due to (alleged infringer's) infringement of (asserted patent(s)). In determining (patent holder's) price-erosion damages, you must also take into account any drop in sales that would have resulted from charging a higher price.

Any price-erosion damages that you award to (patent holder) should be set out separately on the jury verdict form.

Authorities

Power Integrations, Inc. v. Fairchild Semiconductor Int'l, Inc., 711 F.3d 1348, 1378 (Fed. Cir. 2013); *Automated Merch. Sys. v. Crane Co.*, 357 F. App'x 297, 300–01 (Fed. Cir. 2009); *Wechsler v. Macke Int'l Trade, Inc.*, 486 F. 3d 1286, 1293–94 (Fed. Cir. 2007); *compare Crystal Semiconductor Corp. v. Tritech Microelectronics Int'l, Inc.*, 246 F.3d 1336, 1357–58 (Fed. Cir. 2001) (upholding denial of price-erosion damages where patentee failed to show how higher prices would have affected demand for the patented product), with *Ericsson, Inc. v. Harris Corp.*, 352 F.3d 1369, 1377–79 (Fed. Cir. 2003) (upholding award of price-erosion damages where patentee offered sufficient proof of an inelastic market that would support price increases without a drop in sales of the patented product); *see also Vulcan Eng'g Co. v. FATA Aluminum, Inc.*, 278 F.3d 1366, 1377 (Fed. Cir. 2002); *Minco, Inc. v. Combustion Eng'g, Inc.*, 95 F.3d 1109, 1120 (Fed. Cir. 1996); *BIC Leisure Prods., Inc. v. Windsurfing Int'l*, 1 F.3d 1214, 1220 (Fed. Cir. 1993); *3M v. Johnson & Johnson Orthopaedics, Inc.*, 976 F.2d 1559, 1578–79 (Fed. Cir. 1992); *Kalman v. Berlyn Corp.*, 914 F.2d 1473,

1485 (Fed. Cir. 1990); *Amstar Corp. v. Envirotech Corp.*, 823 F.2d 1538, 1543 (Fed. Cir. 1987); *Lam, Inc. v. Johns-Manville Corp.*, 718 F.2d 1056, 1065 (Fed. Cir. 1983).

4.5.9 Lost Profits; Future Lost Profits; Price Erosion

[The following instruction should be given only if the patent holder claims that it should be compensated for future lost profits.]

(Patent holder) may recover additional damages if it proves that (alleged infringer's) infringement of (asserted patent(s)) will cause it to lose profits in the future.

As I have explained to you, you may award price-erosion damages for (patent holder's) sales after it gave notice of its patent rights. You may also consider whether (alleged infringer's) infringement of (asserted patent(s)) will erode the prices at which (patent holder) will be able to sell the product containing the invention in the future.

To recover future lost profits based on this price erosion, (patent holder) must prove that the prices that it will be able to charge for the product containing the invention in the future will be lower than the prices would have been had (alleged infringer) not infringed (asserted patent(s)). If (patent holder) has proven this, future lost profits damages are the difference between:

(1) The amount of profits (patent holder) would have been able to make on future sales at the higher price, and
(2) The amount of profits (patent holder) will actually be able to make on future sales at the lower price.

In determining future lost profits based on this price erosion, you must also consider the effect that higher prices would have on the volume of sales of (patent holder's) products.

Authorities

Shockley v. Arcan, 248 F.3d 1349, 1362 (Fed Cir. 2001) (patentee can recover projected future losses where it "has presented reliable economic evidence of 'but for' causation"); *Fiskars, Inc. v. Hunt Mfg. Co.*, 221 F.3d

1318 (Fed. Cir. 2000) (awarded damages for future losses due to price erosion because it would be difficult for patent holder to raise its prices even after infringement was over); *Oiness v. Walgreen Co.*, 88 F.3d 1025, 1031 (Fed. Cir. 1996) (patentee may recover projected lost profits if supported by sufficient evidence).

4.5.10 Lost Profits; Uncertainties Resolved against Infringer

(Patent holder) must prove its alleged damages and damages cannot be based on speculation or guesswork. Nevertheless, when the amount of the damages cannot be calculated with precision, you must resolve any doubts regarding the amount against (alleged infringer). Any confusion or difficulties caused by (alleged infringer's) failure to keep adequate records should be held against (alleged infringer), not (patent holder).

Authorities

DSU Med. Corp. v. JMS Co., 471 F.3d 1293, 1309 (Fed. Cir. 2006); *Sensonics, Inc. v. Aerosonic Corp.*, 81 F.3d 1566, 1572–73 (Fed. Cir. 1996); *Kalman v. Berlyn Corp.*, 914 F.2d 1473, 1482 (Fed Cir. 1990); *Lam, Inc. v. Johns-Manville Corp.,* 718 F.2d 1056, 1065 (Fed. Cir. 1983); *Story Parchment Co. v. Paterson Parchment Paper Co.*, 282 U.S. 555, 563 (1931).

4.6 Reasonable Royalty; Entitlement; Reasonable Royalty as Alternative to Lost Profits

4.6.1 Amount of Damages

[The following instruction should be given only if the patent holder is seeking damages based on both lost profits and a reasonable royalty.]

(Patent holder) is [also] seeking a reasonable royalty as damages [as an alternative to lost profits damages].

If you find that (patent holder) has proven that (alleged infringer) infringed any valid [and enforceable] claim of (asserted patent(s)), and that (patent holder) has also proven that it is entitled to lost profits damages for all of (alleged infringer's) infringing activities, then the damages that you award to (patent holder) must be only those lost profits, and you must not make any determination about a reasonable royalty. If you find that (patent holder) has not proven that (patent holder) is entitled to any lost profits damages for any of (alleged infringer's) infringing activities, or that (patent holder) is entitled to lost profits damages for only some of (alleged infringer's) infringing activities, then you must determine a reasonable royalty that (patent holder) is entitled to for all of (alleged infringer's) infringing activities for which you have not awarded lost profits damages to (patent holder).

In other words, if (patent holder) has proven that (alleged infringer) infringed any valid [and enforceable] claim of (asserted patent(s)), you must award (patent holder) no less than a reasonable royalty for (alleged infringer's) infringing activities.

As I will explain to you, any amounts of damages that you determine that (patent holder) is entitled to recover based on lost profits or a reasonable royalty must be set out separately on the jury verdict form. The total amount of damages is the sum of any lost profits damages and any reasonable royalty, and this total amount of damages must also be set out separately on the jury verdict form.

Authorities

35 U.S.C. § 284; *Enplas Display Device Corp. v. Seoul Semiconductor Co.*, 909 F.3d 398, 411–12 (Fed. Cir. 2018); *Warsaw Orthopedic, Inc. v. NuVasive, Inc.*, 778 F.3d 1365, 1373–79 (Fed. Cir. 2015), *vacated and remanded by Medtronic Sofamor Danek USA, Inc. v. NuVasive, Inc.*, 136 S. Ct. 893 (2016) (Mem.), *reaff'd in relevant part, Warsaw Orthopedic, Inc. v. NuVasive, Inc.*, 824 F.3d 1344, 1351 (Fed. Cir. 2016); *Siemens Med. Sols. USA, Inc. v. Saint-Gobain Ceramics and Plastics, Inc.*, 637 F.3d 1269, 1288–89 (Fed. Cir. 2011); *Crystal Semiconductor Corp. v. Tritech Microelectronics Int'l, Inc.*, 246 F.3d 1336, 1354 (Fed. Cir. 2001); *State Indus., Inc. v. Mor-Flo Indus., Inc.*, 883 F.2d 1573, 1577 (Fed. Cir. 1989); *Mahurkar v. C.R. Bard, Inc.*, 79 F.3d 1572, 1579 (Fed. Cir. 1996); *Rite-Hite Corp. v. Kelley Co.*, 56 F.3d 1538, 1554 (Fed. Cir. 1995) (en banc).

4.6.2 Reasonable Royalty; Definition

I will now explain to you what a reasonable royalty is. In general, a royalty is a payment that a person makes to a patent holder for the right to [make] [use] [sell] [import] the invention covered by the patent holder's patent. The right to [make] [use] [sell] [import] the invention covered by the patent holder's patent is often called a license. A royalty is also sometimes called a license fee or a license payment. The patent holder is often called the licensor. The person who pays the royalty for the right to [make] [use] [sell] [import] the invention covered by the patent holder's patent is often called the licensee.

A reasonable royalty is the amount of money that a willing licensee would agree to pay, and a willing licensor would agree to accept, for the right to [make] [use] [sell] [import] the invention.

As I will explain to you, there are different ways to determine a reasonable royalty. It is up to you to decide the most appropriate way to determine a reasonable royalty in this case.

Authorities

VirnetX, Inc. v. Cisco Sys., 767 F.3d 1308, 1326 (Fed. Cir. 2014); *Lucent Techs., Inc. v. Gateway, Inc.*, 580 F.3d 1301, 1324–25 (Fed. Cir. 2009); *Rite-Hite Corp. v. Kelley Co.*, 56 F.3d 1538, 1554 (Fed. Cir. 1995) (en banc).

4.6.3 Reasonable Royalty; Form of the Royalty

[The following instruction should be given only if the parties disagree about the form of the reasonable royalty.]

In general, there are two forms that a reasonable royalty may take.

The first form of royalty is a lump-sum payment. In this situation, the licensee makes a single payment to the licensor for the right to [make] [use] [sell] [import] the invention covered by the licensor's patent for the duration of the license.

The second form of royalty is a running royalty. In this situation, the licensee pays a royalty based on the amount of products containing the invention covered by the licensor's patent that the licensee [makes] [uses] [sells] [imports]. A running royalty has two parts—the royalty base and the royalty rate. The royalty base may be a dollar amount, a number of units, or some other quantity. [Based on the evidence presented in this case, the royalty base here must be measured in ( ).]

The royalty rate may be a fixed price per unit, a percentage of the unit price, or some other formula.

In this case, (patent holder) is seeking a lump-sum royalty payment as damages for (alleged infringer's) infringement of (asserted patent(s)). Alternatively, (patent holder) is seeking a running royalty as damages for (alleged infringer's) infringement of (asserted patent(s)).

If you find that (patent holder) has proven that (alleged infringer) infringed any valid [and enforceable] claim of (asserted patent(s)), and that (patent holder) is entitled to a reasonable royalty as damages for (alleged infringer's) infringement of (asserted patent(s)), it is up to you to decide the appropriate way to determine the form of the reasonable royalty in this case: either a lump-sum payment or a running royalty.

Authorities

VirnetX, Inc. v. Cisco Sys., 767 F.3d 1308, 1326 (Fed. Cir. 2014); *LaserDynamics, Inc. v. Quanta Comput., Inc.*, 694 F.3d 51, 69–70 (Fed. Cir. 2012); *Lucent Techs., Inc. v. Gateway, Inc.*, 580 F.3d 1301, 1324, 1338–39 (Fed. Cir. 2009); *Golight, Inc. v. Wal-Mart Stores, Inc.*, 355 F.3d 1327, 1338 (Fed. Cir. 2004); *Mahurkar v. C.R. Bard, Inc.*, 79 F.3d 1572, 1579 (Fed. Cir. 1996); *Rite-Hite Corp. v. Kelley Co.*, 56 F.3d 1538, 1554 (Fed. Cir. 1995) (en banc); *Smithkline Diagnostics, Inc. v. Helena Labs. Corp.*, 926 F.2d 1161, 1167, n.5 (Fed. Cir. 1991).

4.6.4 Reasonable Royalty; Apportionment/Attribution

A product may have more than one component or feature, and some of those components and features may be covered by (asserted patent(s)), while other components and features may not. The amount you find as damages must be based solely on the value attributable to the components and features that are covered by (asserted patent(s)). You must not consider the value of the components or features of (accused product) that are not covered by (asserted patent(s)), the value of (accused product) as a whole, or other factors such as marketing or advertising, or (patent holder's) size or market position.

[IF THE CASE INVOLVES STANDARD-ESSENTIAL PATENTS: If you find that the asserted patent(s) must be used in order to practice the standard, the amount you find as damages must be based solely on the value attributable to the asserted patent(s) and you must not consider the value of the standard as a whole. A holder of a standard-essential patent(s) should only be compensated for the added benefit of its invention. In addition, you must not include any value the patented invention gains because it has become standard essential.]

Authorities

Garretson v. Clark, 111 U.S. 120, 121 (1884); *Bio-Rad Labs., Inc. v. 10X Genomics Inc.*, 967 F.3d 1353, 1371–73 (Fed. Cir. 2020); *Elbit Sys. Land & C4I Ltd. v. Hughes Network Sys., LLC*, 927 F.3d 1292, 1301–02 (Fed. Cir. 2019); *Ericsson, Inc. v. D-Link Sys.*, 773 F.3d 1201, 1226–27, 1232–33 (Fed. Cir. 2014); *VirnetX, Inc. v. Cisco Sys.*, 767 F.3d 1308, 1328–29 (Fed. Cir. 2014); *LaserDynamics, Inc. v. Quanta Comput., Inc.*, 694 F.3d 51, 69–70 (Fed. Cir. 2012); *Uniloc USA, Inc. v. Microsoft Corp.*, 632 F.3d 1292, 1318 (Fed. Cir. 2011); *ResQNet.com, Inc. v. Lansa, Inc.*, 594 F.3d 860, 869 (Fed. Cir. 2010); *Riles v. Shell Exploration & Prod. Co.*, 298 F.3d 1302, 1312 (Fed. Cir. 2002).

4.6.5 Reasonable Royalty; Entire Market Value; Introduction

As I have explained to you, if you find that (accused product) includes components or features that are not covered by (asserted patent(s)), when determining the royalty you must consider only the value of the components or features of (accused product) that are covered by (asserted patent(s)). That is the general rule, though there is an exception to this general rule. I will now explain the exception to that general rule.

Authorities

Synqor, Inc. v. Artesyn Techs., Inc., 709 F.3d 1365, 1383 (Fed. Cir. 2013); *LaserDynamics, Inc. v. Quanta Comput., Inc.*, 694 F.3d 51, 66–68 (Fed. Cir. 2012); *Uniloc USA, Inc. v. Microsoft Corp.*, 632 F.3d 1292, 1318 (Fed. Cir. 2011); *Lucent Techs., Inc. v. Gateway, Inc.*, 580 F.3d 1301, 1336 (Fed. Cir. 2009); *Rite-Hite Corp. v. Kelley Co.*, 56 F.3d 1538, 1549–50 (Fed. Cir. 1995) (en banc); *TWM Mfg. Co. v. Dura Corp.*, 789 F.2d 895, 900–01 (Fed. Cir. 1986).

4.6.6 Reasonable Royalty; Entire Market Value; Customer Demand

The exception to this general rule is when (patent holder) proves the patented feature drives customer demand for the entire multi-component (accused product). However, it is not enough for (patent holder) to show the patented feature is viewed by customers as valuable, important, or even essential to (accused product). Nor is it enough for (patent holder) to show that customers would not want to buy (accused product) without the patented feature. Only if you find that (patent holder) has proven that that patented feature is the basis for the customer demand for the entire multi-component (accused product), may you use the value of (accused product) as a whole when determining the royalty base.

Authorities

Power Integrations, Inc. v. Fairchild Semiconductor Int'l, Inc., 904 F.3d 965, 977–78 (Fed. Cir. 2018); *Astrazeneca AB v. Apotex Corp.*, 782 F.3d 1324, 1338 (Fed. Cir. 2015); *VirnetX, Inc. v. Cisco Sys.*, 767 F.3d 1308, 1326–27 (Fed. Cir. 2014); *Versata Software, Inc. v. SAP Am., Inc.*, 717 F.3d 1255, 1268 (Fed. Cir. 2013); *Synqor, Inc. v. Artesyn Techs., Inc.*, 709 F.3d 1365, 1383 (Fed. Cir. 2013); *LaserDynamics, Inc. v. Quanta Comput., Inc.*, 694 F.3d 51, 66–68 (Fed. Cir. 2012); *Uniloc USA, Inc. v. Microsoft Corp.*, 632 F.3d 1292, 1318 (Fed. Cir. 2011); *Lucent Techs., Inc. v. Gateway, Inc.*, 580 F.3d 1301, 1336 (Fed. Cir. 2009); R*ite-Hite Corp. v. Kelley Co.*, 56 F.3d 1538, 1549–50 (Fed. Cir. 1995) (en banc); *TWM Mfg. Co. v. Dura Corp.*, 789 F.2d 895, 900–01 (Fed. Cir. 1986).

4.6.7 Reasonable Royalty; Hypothetical Negotiation

In general, a reasonable royalty is the amount of money that a reasonable licensee would be willing to pay to a patent holder and that a reasonable patent holder would be willing to receive for a license to the patent holder's patent.

One way to determine a reasonable royalty in this case is to determine what royalty (patent holder) and (alleged infringer) would have agreed to as the result of a hypothetical arm's-length negotiation on the date that (alleged infringer's) allegedly infringing activities started.

For purposes of this hypothetical arm's-length negotiation, you must assume that both (patent holder) and (alleged infringer) would have believed that (asserted patent(s)) is valid. You must also assume that, without a license, (patent holder) and (alleged infringer) would have believed that (alleged infringer's) activities would have infringed (asserted patent(s)).

You must assume that both (patent holder) and (alleged infringer) would have acted reasonably during this hypothetical arm's-length negotiation. You must also assume that (patent holder) and (alleged infringer) would have entered into a license agreement.

You must also keep in mind that the result of this hypothetical arm's-length negotiation would have been a royalty that both (patent holder) and (alleged infringer) would have agreed to under the circumstances, and not necessarily a royalty that either one would have preferred.

In this case, evidence has been presented about events and facts that occurred after the date of this hypothetical arm's-length negotiation. You may consider this evidence if it helps you to determine what reasonable royalty (patent holder) and (alleged infringer) would have agreed to as a result of this hypothetical arm's-length negotiation.

Authorities

Bio-Rad Labs., Inc. v. 10X Genomics Inc., 967 F.3d 1353, 1369 (Fed. Cir. 2020); *VirnetX, Inc. v. Cisco Sys.*, 767 F.3d 1308, 1326 (Fed. Cir. 2014); *LaserDynamics, Inc. v. Quanta Comput., Inc.*, 694 F.3d 51, 70 (Fed. Cir. 2012); *ResQNet.com, Inc. v. Lansa, Inc.*, 594 F.3d 860, 868–73 (Fed. Cir.

2010); *Lucent Techs., Inc. v. Gateway, Inc.*, 580 F.3d 1301, 1324–25 (Fed. Cir. 2009); *Rite-Hite Corp. v. Kelley Co.*, 56 F.3d 1538, 1554 (Fed. Cir. 1995) (en banc); *Georgia-Pacific Corp. v. United States Plywood Corp.*, 318 F. Supp. 1116, 1120 (S.D.N.Y. 1970), judgment modified by 446 F.2d 295 (2d Cir. 1971); Jury Charge, ECF No. 562, *Summit 6 LLC v. Research in Motion Corp.*, 3:11-cv-00367-O at 39 (N.D. Tex. April 5, 2013).

4.6.8 Reasonable Royalty; Hypothetical Negotiation; Non-Exclusive Factors

You may consider the following list of factors when determining a reasonable royalty. This list is not intended to be exhaustive or exclusive. You may consider all of the evidence presented at trial when determining a reasonable royalty.

[Only the factors that are relevant to the case should be described.]

(1) The royalties received by the patentee for the licensing of the patent(s)-in-suit.
(2) The rates paid by the licensee for the use of other patents comparable to the patent(s)-in-suit.
(3) The nature and scope of the license, as exclusive or nonexclusive, or as restricted or nonrestricted in terms of territory or with respect to the parties to whom the product may be sold.
(4) The licensor's established policy and marketing program to maintain his or her patent monopoly by not licensing others to use the invention or by granting licenses under special conditions designed to preserve that monopoly.
(5) The commercial relationship between the licensor and licensee, such as whether they are competitors in the same territory in the same line of business, or whether they are inventor and promoter.
(6) The effect of selling the patented specialty in promoting sales of other products of the licensee, the existing value of the invention to the licensor as a generator of sales of his nonpatented items, and the extent of such derivative or convoyed sales.
(7) The duration of the patent and the term of the license.

(8) The established profitability of the product made under the patents, its commercial success, and its current popularity.
(9) The utility and advantages of the patented property over the old modes or devices, if any, that had been used for working out similar results.
(10) The nature of the patented invention, the character of the commercial embodiment of it as owned and produced by the licensor, and the benefits to those who have used the invention.
(11) The extent to which the infringer has made use of the invention and any evidence probative of the value of that use.
(12) The portion of the profit or of the selling price that may be customary in the particular business or in comparable business to allow for the use of the invention or analogous inventions.
(13) The portion of the realizable profits that should be credited to the invention as distinguished from nonpatented elements, the manufacturing process, business risks, or significant features or improvements added by the infringer.
(14) The opinion and testimony of qualified experts.
(15) The amount that a licensor (such as the patentee) and a licensee (such as the infringer) would have agreed upon (at the time the infringement began) if both had been reasonably and voluntarily trying to reach an agreement; that is, the amount which a prudent licensee—who desired, as a business proposition, to obtain a license to manufacture and sell a particular article embodying the patented invention—would have been willing to pay as a royalty and yet be able to make a reasonable profit and which amount would have been acceptable by a prudent patentee who was willing to grant a license.

To repeat, when determining a reasonable royalty, you need not consider all of these factors, and these factors are not the only factors that you may consider. They are only a guide to assist you when determining a reasonable royalty. However, if you choose to rely upon evidence from any other license agreements, you must account for any differences between those licenses and the hypothetically negotiated license in terms of the technologies and economic circumstances of the contracting parties.

Note

The Federal Circuit has never adopted or described the *Georgia-Pacific* factors as "a talisman for royalty rate *calculations*." *Ericsson, Inc. v. D-Link Sys.*, 773 F.3d 1201, 1230–31 (Fed. Cir. 2014). Thus, testifying witnesses are permitted to use any or all of those factors, in addition to other factors, when testifying about damages. *WhitServe, LLC v. Comput. Packages, Inc.*, 694 F.3d 10, 31–32 (Fed. Cir. 2012). The jury is also permitted to consider any, all, or none of the *Georgia-Pacific* factors as well as other evidence presented when determining a reasonable royalty. *See id.* However, if the *Georgia-Pacific* factors are used, the jury should be instructed only on the factors that are relevant to the evidence before the jury. *Ericsson, Inc. v. D-Link Sys.*, 773 F.3d 1201, 1231 (Fed. Cir. 2014) (stating that "the district court erred by instructing the jury on multiple *Georgia-Pacific* factors that are not relevant, or are misleading, on the record before it").

If licenses based on the entire value of a multi-component product are admitted or referenced in expert testimony, the jury should receive a cautionary instruction regarding the limited purposes for which such testimony is proffered if the accused infringer requests the instruction. *Ericsson, Inc. v. D-Link Sys.*, 773 F.3d 1201, 1228 (Fed. Cir. 2014).

If one or more asserted patents is alleged to be FRAND-encumbered, the list of *Georgia-Pacific* factors may be revised to fit the FRAND context. For example, in *Ericsson, Inc. v. D-Link Sys.*, 773 F.3d 1201, 1231 (Fed. Cir. 2014), a panel of the Federal Circuit Court of Appeals held that "at least [*Georgia-Pacific* factors] 4, 5, 8, 9 and 10" were irrelevant or misleading in a FRAND context on the record before it. The panel did not "address whether shifting the timing of the hypothetical negotiation is either appropriate or necessary," such as to the date of the adoption of the technical standard. *See Ericsson*, 773 F.3d at 1234 n.10. As FRAND obligations vary among standard-setting organizations, and the Federal Circuit has held that, because "'[F]RAND terms' vary from case to case," specific instructions on determining the patent holder's obligations are not provided here; the trial court must instruct the jury on the patent holder's actual FRAND commitments and it is left to the parties to craft an instruction that adequately does so. *Id.* at 1231, 1235.

Authorities

Bio-Rad Labs., Inc. v. 10X Genomics Inc., 967 F.3d 1353, 1370 (Fed. Cir. 2020); *Summit 6, LLC v. Samsung Elecs. Co.*, 802 F.3d 1283, 1296 (Fed. Cir. 2015); *Astrazeneca AB v. Apotex Corp.*, 782 F.3d 1324, 1336 (Fed. Cir. 2015); *Ericsson, Inc. v. D-Link Sys.*, 773 F.3d 1201, 1227, 1230–31 (Fed. Cir. 2014); *Apple, Inc. v. Motorola, Inc.*, 757 F.3d 1286, 1325–26 (Fed. Cir. 2014), overruled on other grounds by *Williamson v. Citrix Online, LLC*, 792 F.3d 1339 (Fed. Cir. 2015) (en banc); *Energy Transp. Grp., Inc. v. William Demant Holding A/S*, 697 F.3d 1342, 1357 (Fed. Cir. 2012); *Whitserve, LLC v. Comput. Packages, Inc.*, 694 F.3d 10, 31 (Fed. Cir. 2012); *In re MSTG, Inc.*, 675 F.3d 1337, 1348 (Fed. Cir. 2012); *ResQNet.com, Inc. v. Lansa, Inc.*, 594 F.3d 860, 870 (Fed. Cir. 2010); *Lucent Techs., Inc. v. Gateway, Inc.*, 580 F.3d 1301, 1324 (Fed. Cir. 2009); *Mars, Inc. v. Coin Acceptors, Inc.*, 527 F.3d 1359, 1372–73 (Fed. Cir. 2008); *Riles v. Shell Expl. & Prod. Co.*, 298 F.3d 1302, 1312 (Fed. Cir. 2002); *Grain Processing Corp. v. American Maize-Prod. Co.*, 185 F.3d 1341, 1349 (Fed. Cir. 1999); *Georgia-Pacific Corp. v. United States Plywood Corp.*, 318 F. Supp. 1116, 1120 (S.D.N.Y. 1970), judgment modified by 446 F.2d 295 (2d Cir. 1971).

4.6.9 Reasonable Royalty; "Patent Hold-Up" and "Royalty Stacking"; FRAND

[The following instruction should be given only if the alleged infringer has introduced evidence of "patent hold-up" or "royalty stacking."]

If you find that (asserted patent(s)) is a standard-essential patent, and that (patent holder) committed to grant licenses to others on fair, reasonable, and non-discriminatory (or FRAND) terms, then you must determine a reasonable royalty for damages for (alleged infringer's) infringing activities. There are two additional factors that you must consider when determining a FRAND royalty: patent hold-up and royalty stacking.

When a patent must be used to comply with a technical standard, the patent holder of the patent is in a position to "hold up" or prevent another person from complying with the technical standard. In this situation, the patent holder could demand a higher royalty to license its standard-essential patent than the patent holder would otherwise be able to license its patent for if it were not standard-essential. This is called "patent hold-up."

When a technical standard includes more than one standard-essential patent, each holder of a standard-essential patent could demand a royalty for the use of its patent. In such a situation, the royalties for all of the standard-essential patents would then "stack" one on top of the other and the total of all the royalties for all of the patents that are essential to the standard could be excessive. This is called "royalty stacking."

If you find that (patent holder) committed to grant licenses to (asserted patent(s)) on FRAND terms, that commitment is designed, in part, to prevent both "patent hold-up" and "royalty stacking." You should not award a reasonable royalty that includes value attributable to patent hold-up. Moreover, your reasonable royalty should take into account the potential for royalty stacking.

Authorities

Microsoft Corp. v. Motorola, Inc., 795 F.3d 1024, 1030–31 (9th Cir. 2015); *Ericsson, Inc. v. D-Link Sys.*, 773 F.3d 1201, 1209, 1234–35 (Fed. Cir. 2014); *Lotes Co., Ltd. v. Hon Hai Precision Indus. Co., Ltd.*, 753 F.3d 395, 400 (2d Cir. 2014); *Qualcomm Inc. v. Broadcom Corp.*, 548 F.3d 1004, 1010 (Fed. Cir. 2008); *Broadcom Corp. v. Qualcomm Inc.*, 501 F.3d 297, 310 (3d Cir. 2007).

Further authorities related to FRAND include: *Apple, Inc. v. Motorola, Inc.*, 757 F.3d 1286, 1323–26 (Fed. Cir. 2014), *overruled on other grounds by Williamson v. Citrix Online*, 792 F.3d 1339 (Fed. Cir. 2015) (en banc); *Rambus Inc. v. FTC*, 522 F.3d 456, 462 (D.C. Cir. 2008).

4.7 Induced Infringement

If you find that (alleged infringer) induced one or more other persons to [make] [use] [sell] the invention covered by (asserted patent(s)), and thereby caused those other persons to infringe (asserted patent(s)), you must award damages to (patent holder) to compensate (patent holder) for those infringing activities.

However, when determining the amount of damages to award to (patent holder) based on induced infringement, you must keep in mind that damages for induced infringement are limited to the damages for each act of direct infringement. Therefore, any damages awarded to (patent holder) because (alleged infringer) induced one or more other persons to [make] [use] [sell] the patented invention, and thereby caused those other persons to infringe (asserted patent(s)), must be based on each act of direct infringement.

Authorities

Syngenta Crop Prot., LLC v. Willowood, LLC, 944 F.3d 1344, 1361–63 (Fed. Cir. 2019) *cert. denied*, 2020 WL 5882228 (Oct. 5, 2020) (No. 19-1147); *Finjan, Inc. v. Proofpoint, Inc.*, No. 13-cv-05808-HSG, 2015 WL 1517920, at *12 (N.D. Cal. Apr. 2, 2015); *Limelight Networks, Inc. v. Akamai Techs., Inc.*, 572 U.S. 915, 920–22 (2014); *Cardiac Pacemakers, Inc. v. St. Jude Med., Inc.*, 576 F.3d 1348, 1363 (Fed. Cir. 2009); *Dynacore Holdings Corp. v. U.S. Philips Corp.*, 363 F.3d 1263, 1272 (Fed. Cir. 2004).

4.8 Contributory Infringement

If you find that (alleged infringer) contributed to the infringement of (asserted patent(s)) by one or more other persons, you must award damages to (patent holder) to compensate (patent holder) for those infringing activities.

However, when determining the amount of damages to award to (patent holder) based on any contributory infringement, you must keep in mind that damages for contributory infringement are limited to the damages for each act of direct infringement. Therefore, any damages awarded to (patent holder) because (alleged infringer) contributed to the infringement of (asserted patent(s)) by one or more other persons must be based on each act of direct infringement.

Authorities

Finjan, Inc. v. Proofpoint, Inc., No. 13-cv-05808-HSG, 2015 WL 1517920, at *12 (N.D. Cal. Apr. 2, 2015); *Limelight Networks, Inc. v. Akamai Techs., Inc.*, 572 U.S. 915, 920–22 (2014); *Cardiac Pacemakers, Inc. v. St. Jude Med., Inc.*, 576 F.3d 1348 (Fed. Cir. 2009); *Lucent Techs., Inc. v. Gateway, Inc.*, 580 F.3d 1301, 1323–24, 1334 (Fed. Cir. 2009); *Dynacore Holdings Corp. v. U.S. Philips Corp.*, 363 F.3d 1263 (Fed. Cir. 2004).

4.9 Design Patents; Damages

4.9.1 Design Patent Damages; Generally

I will instruct you about the measure of damages for infringement of (patent holder's) design patents. By instructing you on damages, I am not suggesting which party should win on any issue.

If you find (alleged infringer(s)) infringed any valid (patent holder) design patent, you must then determine the money damages to award (patent holder). The amount of those damages must be adequate to compensate (patent holder) for the infringement. You should keep in mind that the damages you award are meant to compensate the patent holder and not to punish an infringer.

In relation to design patents, (patent holder) can elect to prove either actual damages, known as compensatory damages, or it may elect to prove the (alleged infringer's) profits as its measure of potential recovery with respect to the sale of each unit of an infringing product. As compensatory damages, (patent holder) may prove either its own lost profits, or a reasonable royalty for the design patent.

Lost profits consist of any actual reduction in business profits (patent owner) suffered as result of (alleged infringer's) alleged infringement of the (asserted patent) design patent. A reasonable royalty is defined as the amount (patent owner) and someone wanting to use the patented design would agree upon as a fee for use of the design, I will describe shortly what (patent owner) must prove to recover each type of damages.

(Patent owner) is entitled to recover no less than a reasonable royalty for each infringing [sale] [offer for sale] [use] [importation], even if (patent owner) cannot prove that it suffered lost profits in connection with that [sale] [offer for sale] [use] [importation].

(Patent holder) is not entitled to recover both compensatory damages and (alleged infringer's) profits on the same [sale] [offer for sale] [use] [importation]. Further, your damages determination must not include additional sums to punish (alleged infringer) or to set an example.

Authorities

35 U.S.C. §§ 284, 289; *Catalina Lighting v. Lamps Plus*, 295 F.3d 1277, 1290–92 (Fed. Cir. 2002); *Rite-Hite Corp. v. Kelley Co.*, 56 F.3d 1538, 1544–45 (Fed. Cir. 1995) (en banc).

4.9.2 Burden of Proof

(Patent holder) has the burden to prove that (patent holder's) calculation of damages is correct by a preponderance of the evidence. That is, the party with the burden of proof must show that the fact is more likely true than not true. While (patent holder) is not required to prove its damages with mathematical precision, it must prove them with reasonable certainty. (Patent holder) is not entitled to damages that are remote or speculative.

Authorities

Wechsler v. Macke Int'l Trade, Inc., 486 F.3d 1286, 1293–94 (Fed. Cir. 2007); *Grain Processing Corp. v. Am. Maize-Prod. Co.*, 185 F.3d 1341, 1349 (Fed. Cir. 1999) (plaintiff must prove the amount of its lost profits by a reasonable probability); *Rite-Hite Corp. v. Kelley Co.*, 56 F.3d 1538, 1545 (Fed. Cir. 1995) (en banc) (same); *Oiness v. Walgreen Co.*, 88 F.3d 1025, 1030–31 (Fed. Cir. 1996) (the amount of lost profits cannot be based on mere speculation or guess); *Smithkline Diagnostics, Inc. v. Helena Labs. Corp.*, 926 F.2d 1161, 1164 n.2 (Fed. Cir. 1991) (same); *Lam, Inc. v. Johns-Manville Corp.*, 718 F.2d 1056, 1065 (Fed. Cir. 1983) (doubts resulting from defendant's failure to retain appropriate records are to be resolved in the plaintiff's favor); *Ryco, Inc. v. Ag-Bag Corp.*, 857 F.2d 1418, 1428 (Fed. Cir. 1988); *Del Mar Avionics, Inc. v. Quinton Instrument Co.*, 836 F.2d 1320, 1327 (Fed. Cir. 1987) (mathematical certainty is not required).

4.9.3 Lost Profits

[If ONLY design patents are asserted, and thus the utility patent instructions contained above have not been provided to the jury, provide the lost profits instructions for utility patents above, replacing references to utility patents with design patents, references to patented invention with patented design, and references to patented products or products covered by a patent claim with products or articles that use or embody the patented design. DO NOT provide the below instruction unless utility patents are also asserted.]

I have explained to you how to determine damages based on (patent holder's) lost profits and based on a reasonable royalty in relation to utility patents. In assessing (patent holder's) right to recover lost profits for (alleged infringer(s)'s) infringement of its design patents, you should apply the same rules I have already explained in the context of lost profits for infringement of (patent holder's) utility patents.

Wherever in those instructions I referred to (patent holder's) utility patents, you should now focus on (patent holder's) design patents. Wherever in those instructions I referred to the patented invention, you should now focus on the patented design. Wherever in those instructions I referred to patented products or products covered by a patent claim, you should now focus on products or articles that use or embody the patented design.

Authorities

35 U.S.C. § 284; *Wechsler v. Macke Int'l Trade, Inc.*, 486 F.3d 1286, 1293–94 (Fed. Cir. 2007); *Ericsson, Inc. v. Harris Corp.*, 352 F.3d 1369, 1377–79 (Fed. Cir. 2003); *Ferguson Beauregard/Logic Controls, Div. of Dover Res., Inc. v. Mega Sys., LLC*, 350 F.3d 1327, 1345–46 (Fed. Cir. 2003); *Micro Chem., Inc. v. Lextron, Inc.*, 318 F.3d 1119, 1122–23 (Fed. Cir. 2003);

Crystal Semiconductor Corp. v. Tritech Microelectronics Int'l, Inc., 246 F.3d 1336, 1353–61 (Fed. Cir. 2001); *Rite-Hite Corp. v. Kelley Co.*, 56 F.3d 1538, 1545 (Fed. Cir. 1995) (en banc), *State Indus., Inc. v. Mor-Flo Indus., Inc.*, 883 F.2d 1573, 1576–80 (Fed. Cir. 1989); *Central Soya Co. v. Geo. A. Hormel & Co.*, 723 F.2d 1573, 1578–80 (Fed. Cir. 1983); *Paper Converting Mach. Co. v. Magna-Graphics Corp.*, 745 F.2d 11, 22 (Fed. Cir. 1984) (the proper measure of recovery is any net profits lost by plaintiff as a result of defendant's infringing acts, while the plaintiff's fixed costs are generally ignored in determining those incremental profits); *Lam, Inc. v. Johns-Manville Corp.*, 718 F.2d 1056, 1065 (Fed. Cir. 1983); *Panduit Corp. v Stahlin Bros. Fibre Works*, 575 F.2d 1152, 1156 (6th Cir. 1978); *Aro Mfg. Co. v. Convertible Top Replacement Co., Inc.*, 377 U.S. 476, 507–10 (1964).

4.9.4 Reasonable Royalty

[If ONLY design patents are asserted, and thus the utility patent instructions contained above have not been provided to the jury, provide the reasonable royalty instructions for utility patents above, replacing references to utility patents with design patents, references to patented invention with patented design, and references to patented products or products covered by a patent claim with products or articles that use or embody the patented design. DO NOT provide the below instruction unless utility patents are also asserted.]

I have likewise already explained to you how to determine damages based on a reasonable royalty in relation to utility patents. If (patent holder) has not proven its claim for lost profits, or has not proven its claim to (alleged infringer(s)'s) profits, which I will discuss next, then (patent holder) should be awarded a reasonable royalty for all infringing sales by (alleged infringer(s)). In no event should the damages you award (patent holder) for design patent infringement be less than a reasonable royalty.

The definition of a reasonable royalty for design patent infringement is the same as the definition I explained to you for utility patent infringement. However, wherever in that instruction I referred to the patented invention or a utility patent, you should now focus on design patents or patented designs.

Authorities

35 U.S.C. § 284; *Golight, Inc. v. Wal-Mart Stores, Inc.*, 355 F.3d 1327, 1338 (Fed. Cir. 2004); *Crystal Semiconductor Corp. v. Tritech Microetlectronics Int'l, Inc.*, 246 F.3d 1336, 1353–54 (Fed. Cir. 2001); *Fromson v. W. Litho Plate & Supply Co.*, 853 F.2d 1568, 1574–76 (Fed. Cir. 1988) (overruled on other grounds); *Minco, Inc. v. Combustion Eng'g, Inc.*, 95 F.3d 1109, 1119–20 (Fed. Cir. 1996); *Mahurkar v. C.R. Bard, Inc.*, 79 F.3d 1572, 1579–81 (Fed. Cir. 1996); *Maxwell v. J. Baker, Inc.*, 86 F.3d 1098, 1108–10 (Fed. Cir. 1996); *Rite-Hite Corp. v. Kelley Co.*, 56 F.3d 1538, 1554 (Fed. Cir. 1995) (en banc). The factors to be considered originated in *Georgia-Pacific Corp. v. United States Plywood Corp.*, 318 F. Supp. 1116, 1120 (S.D.N.Y. 1970).

4.9.5 (Alleged Infringer's) Profits

I will now explain to you how to determine damages based on (alleged infringer(s)'s) total profit.

In this case, (patent holder) seeks (alleged infringer(s)'s) profits from sales of products alleged to infringe (patent holder's) design patents. If you find infringement by (alleged infringer(s)) and do not find (patent holder's) design patents are invalid, you may award (patent holder) (alleged infringer(s)'s) total profit attributable to the infringing products. A design patent owner can recover the profit not only of the manufacturer or producer of an infringing article, but also of other sellers in the chain of distribution.

(Alleged infringer's) "total profit" is the entire profit on the sales of (accused product(s)) to which the patented design is applied or with which the patented design is used. Total profit is not only the portion of profit attributable to the design or ornamental aspects of (accused product(s)). However, "total profit" does not include profit attributable to other products (alleged infringer(s)) may have sold with (accused product(s)).

If you find infringement by (alleged infringer(s)), (patent holder) is entitled to all profit earned by (alleged infringer(s)) on sales of articles that infringe (patent holder's) design patent(s). Total profit is determined by deducting certain expenses from gross revenue. Therefore, to determine (alleged infringer(s)'s) total profit, you must start by determining (alleged infringer(s)'s) gross revenue.

(Alleged infringer(s)'s) gross revenue is the money that (alleged infringer) received from infringing sales. (Patent holder) has the burden of proving (alleged infringer(s)'s) gross revenue by a preponderance of the evidence.

Next, you must determine (alleged infringer(s)'s) expenses incurred to make the infringing sales. (Alleged infringer(s)'s) expenses can include costs incurred by (alleged infringer(s)) in producing the gross revenue, such as the cost of goods. Therefore, to determine (alleged infringer(s)'s) total profit, you must, for example, deduct (alleged infringer(s)'s) cost of goods from (alleged infringer(s)'s) gross revenue.

In determining (alleged infringer(s)'s) total profit, other expenses incurred by (alleged infringer(s)) may be deducted from (alleged infringer(s)'s) gross revenue if they are directly attributable to infringing sales. (Alleged infringer(s)) has the burden of proving what expenses are directly attributable to infringing sales.

Authorities

35 U.S.C. §§ 171(a), 289; *Samsung Elecs. Co. v. Apple, Inc.*, 137 S. Ct. 429, 432–35 (2016); *Catalina Lighting v. Lamps Plus*, 295 F.3d 1277, 1291–92 (Fed. Cir. 2002); *Nike Inc. v. Wal-Mart Stores, Inc.*, 138 F.3d 1437, 1441, 1447–48 (Fed. Cir. 1998); *Braun, Inc. v. Dynamics Corp. of Am.*, 975 F.2d 815, 824 (Fed. Cir. 1992); *Trans-World Mfg. Corp. v. A1 Nyman & Sons, Inc.*, 750 F.2d 1552, 1566–68 (Fed. Cir. 1984).

Note

A patent holder is entitled to recover either its lost profits and/or a reasonable royalty, or the infringer's profits. If a patent holder seeks lost profits and/or a reasonable royalty, or the infringer's profits in the alternative, the jury should be instructed that it can award only one type of damage on each sale—either (1) the patent holder's lost profits or a reasonable royalty or (2) the infringer's profits on the relevant article of manufacture. *Nordock, Inc. v. Sys. Inc.*, 681 F. App'x 965, 966 (Fed. Cir. 2017) (nonprecedential).

For a discussion of what constitutes an article of manufacture, *see Samsung Elecs. Co., Ltd. v. Apple, Inc.*, 137 S. Ct. 429, 434–36 (2016).

4.9.6 Date Damages Begin

[Note: The following instruction should be given in the event the parties agree on the date for commencement of damages.]

In this case, you should assess damages/the right to recover (alleged infringer's) profits beginning on [date]. (Patent owner) and (alleged infringer) have agreed upon this date.

[Note: The following instruction should be given in the event the parties agree that the marking requirement was satisfied or does not apply.]

In this case, if you find that the (asserted patent(s)) design patent(s) was granted before the infringing activity began, you should calculate damages as of the date you determine that the infringement began. If you find that the (asserted patent(s)) design patent(s) was granted after the infringement began, damages should be calculated as of [date patent issued].

[Note: The following instruction should be given if marking is at issue.]

The amount of damages that (patent holder) may be awarded by you is limited to those acts of infringement by (alleged infringer) that occurred after (patent owner) gave (alleged infringer) notice that it infringed the (asserted patent) design patent. Notice of infringement can be actual or constructive, and I will explain in a moment what that means.

One way (patent holder) could have given notice of its patent rights is by giving actual notice to (alleged infringer). (Patent holder) could have given actual notice to (alleged infringer) by notifying (alleged infringer) that (alleged infringer) was allegedly infringing (asserted patent(s)) and by identifying (alleged infringer's) products that allegedly infringed (asserted patent(s)). This way of actual notice to (alleged infringer) is effective on the date that it was given to (alleged infringer).

The other way that (patent holder) could have given notice of its patent rights, called "constructive notice," is by giving notice to the general public by marking products it [made] [used] [sold] [imported] with the word "Patent" or the abbreviation "Pat." and the number of (the asserted patent(s)) or a free internet address that associates (patent holder's) products with the patent number of (asserted patent(s)). The free internet address may be listed on the product packaging or label if not feasible to list it on the actual product. This way of notice to the general public is on the date that (patent holder) started to mark substantially all of the products that contain the invention covered by (asserted patent(s)) in that manner.

The burden is on (patent holder) to show that it has marked its products. In addition to marking substantially all of its products that contain the invention covered by the asserted patent(s), once marking has begun, it must be substantially continuous. If (alleged infringer) identifies any unmarked products that it alleges should have been marked, (patent holder) bears the burden of proving that those products did not need to be marked. Further, if the patent holder has made or sold patented articles that were not marked, damages do not accrue until (patent holder) provided actual notice of the patents.

If (patent holder) has licensed the asserted patent(s) and the licensee makes or sells a patented article, then the requirement to mark extends to the licensee. To satisfy the marking requirement where a licensee and not the patent holder makes or sells a patented article, (patent holder) must have made reasonable efforts to ensure its licensee complied with the marking requirement.

To summarize, (patent holder) is entitled to recover damages only for infringement that occurred after (patent holder) gave notice of its patent rights by either marking (patent holder's) products or by giving actual notice to (alleged infringer), as I have just explained.

If you find that (patent holder) sells products that include the claimed designs but has not marked those products with the patent numbers, you must determine the date that each (alleged infringer(s)) received actual written notice of the patents and the specific products alleged to infringe.

On the other hand, if you find that (patent holder) does not sell products covered by a patent, then damages begin without the requirement for actual notice under the following circumstances:

- For each infringed patent that was granted before the infringing activity began, damages should be calculated as of the date you determine infringement began; or
- For each infringed patent that was granted after the infringing activity began as determined by you, damages should be calculated as of the date the patent issued.

Authorities

35 U.S.C. § 287; *Crown Packaging Tech., Inc. v. Rexam Bev. Can Co.*, 559 F.3d 1308, 1316–17 (Fed. Cir. 2009); *State Contr. & Eng'g Corp. v. Condotte Am., Inc.*, 346 F.3d 1057, 1073–74 (Fed. Cir. 2003); *Crystal Semiconductor Corp. v. Tritech Microelectronics Int'l, Inc.*, 246 F.3d 1336, 1353 (Fed. Cir. 2001); *Gart v. Logitech, Inc.*, 254 F.3d 1334, 1345–47 (Fed. Cir. 2001); *Maxwell v. J. Baker, Inc.*, 86 F.3d 1098, 1111 (Fed. Cir. 1996); *Amsted Indus. v. Buckeye Steel Castings Co.*, 24 F.3d 178, 187–88 (Fed. Cir. 1994).

Chapter Five

SAMPLE JURY VERDICT FORM

INTRODUCTION

When completing this jury verdict form, you must follow all the instructions I have given you in the court's final jury instructions. You should follow the directions provided throughout the form. Your response to each part of this jury verdict form must be unanimous.

Some parts of this jury verdict form contain terms that were explained to you during the jury instructions. You should refer to the explanations in the jury instructions whenever you have a question about the meaning of a term in this jury verdict form.

JURY VERDICT FORM

Question No. 1:

Did (patent holder) prove by a preponderance of the evidence that (alleged infringer) infringed one or more of the claims of the asserted patent(s)?

[Asserted patent, asserted claim] Yes: ______ No: _____

[Repeat for each asserted claim of each asserted patent.]

Question No. 2:

Did (alleged infringer) prove by clear and convincing evidence that one or more claims of the asserted patent(s) is invalid?

[Asserted patent, asserted claim] Yes: ______ No: _____

[Repeat for each asserted claim of each asserted patent.]

If you answered NO for all asserted claims in Question No. 1, OR answered YES for all asserted claims in Question No. 2, then DO NOT answer Question No. 3.

Answer Question No. 3 ONLY as to any asserted claim that you have found to be BOTH infringed (YES to Question 1) AND not invalid (NO to Question 2).

Question No. 3:

Did (patent holder) prove by a preponderance of the evidence that (alleged infringer) willfully infringed ANY of the asserted claims you found were infringed?

Yes: ______ No: _____

If you answered NO for all asserted claims in Question No. 1, OR answered YES for all asserted claims in Question No. 2, then DO NOT answer Question No. 4(a).

Answer Question No. 4(a) ONLY as to any asserted claim that you have found to be BOTH infringed AND not invalid.

Question 4(a):

What sum of money, if any, did (patent holder) prove by a preponderance of the evidence that it is entitled to as lost profits?

$________________________________

If you awarded lost profits in Question 4(a), you must also answer Question 4(b) as to any acts of infringement for which you have not already awarded lost profits.

If you did NOT award any lost profits in Question 4(a), you must answer Question 4(b) as to ALL acts of infringement.

Question 4(b):

What sum of money, if any, did (patent holder) prove by a preponderance of the evidence would compensate (patent holder) as a reasonable royalty for its damages resulting from (alleged infringer's) infringement? (You may award ONLY a lump-sum amount or a running-royalty amount, NOT both.)

$____ (Lump Sum)

OR

Royalty Base (____________) × Royalty Rate (______) = $____________ (Running Royalty)

If you awarded lost profits in Question 4(a), and a reasonable royalty in Question 4(b), answer Question 4(c).

Question 4(c):

Calculate the total amount of damages you have found that (patent holder) is entitled to:

(a) Lost Profits Damages $____________
(insert amount from Question 4(a))

(b) Reasonable Royalty Damages $____________
(insert amount from Question 4(b))

TOTAL DAMAGES (add (a) and (b)) $____________

You have now completed this Jury Verdict Form. Please review all of your responses to ensure that they are complete and that they accurately reflect your unanimous determinations. The Jury Foreperson should then sign and date this Jury Verdict Form in the spaces below and notify the bailiff that you have reached a unanimous verdict. The Jury Foreperson should retain possession of the Jury Verdict Form and bring it with [him] [her] when the jury is brought back into the courtroom.

DATED: ________________ By: ______________________________

Jury Foreperson

NOTE

This sample jury verdict form assumes a case in which infringement and validity are contested, where both lost profits and a reasonable royalty are claimed, and where a reasonable royalty can only be awarded in the form of a lump sum or a running royalty (not both). The form and substance of the questions on a verdict form will vary based on the particular facts and circumstances of each case, the relevant case law, and the parties' positions.

Table of Cases

A

G

H

I

J

K

L

M

O

P

Q

R

Index

V

W